Truth of My Songs:
Poems of the Trobairitz

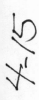

Truth of My Songs:
Poems of the Trobairitz
Translated and with an introduction by
Claudia Keelan

OMNIDAWN PUBLISHING
RICHMOND, CALIFORNIA
2015

Original cover art: *Allegro Moderato* © Aleksei Tivetsky and Elena Moross.
Courtesy of the artist.

Book cover and interior design by Cassandra Smith

Cover and interior text set in Warnock Pro.

Each Omnidawn author participates fully in the design of her or his
book, choosing cover art and approving cover and interior design.
Omnidawn strives to create books that align with each author's vision.

Offset printed in the United States
by Edwards Brothers Malloy, Ann Arbor, Michigan
On 55# Enviro Natural 100% Recycled 100% PCW
Acid Free Archival Quality FSC Certified Paper
with Rainbow FSC Certified Colored End Papers

Library of Congress Cataloging-in-Publication Data

Truth of my songs : poems of the Trobairitz / translated and with an
    introduction by Claudia Keelan.
    pages cm
ISBN 978-1-63243-002-1 (pbk. : alk. paper)
1. Provençal poetry--Translations into English. 2. Provençal poetry--
    Women authors. 3. Troubadours. I. Keelan, Claudia, 1959-
PC3366.E5T78 2015
849'.120809287--dc23

                                        2014040741

Published by Omnidawn Publishing, Richmond, California
www.omnidawn.com   (510) 237-5472   (800) 792-4957
                10 9 8 7 6 5 4 3 2 1
                ISBN: 978-1-63243-002-1

Thanks to *New American Writing, The Offending Adam, Transom, Volt* and *Witness* where some of these translations first appeared.

Contents

Introduction:
Is You Is, Or Is You Ain't My Baby? Finding the
Trobairitz   11

Anonymous
En un vergier sotz fuella d' albespi   36
Under the Green Leaves of the Thorn Tree   37

Almucs de Castelnau and Iseut de Capio
Dompna n' Almucs, si. us plages   38
Girlfriend, I'm begging, Don't Be Rude   39

Castelloza
Ja de chantar non degr' aver talan   40
I Should Give Up on Song   41

Amics, s' ie. us trobes avinen   44
If You'd Shown Just a Little Care   45

Mout avetz faich long estatge   48
You Stayed for Days and Nights   49

Anonymous
Coindeta sui...   52
I Am so Pretty...   53

Alais, Iselda, and Carenza
Na Carenza al bel cors avinen   54
Lady C., Your Body is a Form of Light   55

Anonymous
Ab greu cossire   56
I Grew Coarse   57

Raimbaut D'Aurenga and Anonymous Domna
Amics, en gran cossirier   60
So, Amigo, I'm Bankrupt   61

RAIMON DE LAS SALAS AND ANONYMOUS DOMNA
Si. m. fors graziz mos chanz, eu m' esforcera   64
If I could feel some gratitude I'd sing   65

ANONYMOUS
Quan vei los praz verdesir   68
When I See the Fields Go Green   69

GUILLELMA DE ROSERS AND LANFRANCS CIGALA
Na Guillelma, man cavalier arratge   72
It was a Cold and Stormy Night   73

GARSENDA AND GUI DE CAVAILLON
Vos que. m semblatz dels corals amadors   76
You So Blubber in My Luver Junk   77

GUILLEM RAINOL D'AT AND ANONYMOUS DOMNA
Quant aug chantar lo gal sus en l' erbos   78
When I hear the Cock Crow in the Parks   79

ANONYMOUS
Quant lo gilos es fora   80
When the Husband is Away   81

COMTESSA OR BEATRIZ DE DIA
Ab joi et joven m' apais   82
I Keep My Thrive Alive by Youth and Joy   83

A chantar m' er de so qu' ieu non volria   86
I Sing of Things Better Left Unsaid   87

Estat ai en greu cossirier   88
I've Been Thrown into Hell   89

Fin ioi me don' alegranssa   90
True Love Carries Its Share of Joy   91

ANONYMOUS
A l' entrade del tens clar   92
At the Start of Spring   93

ALAMANDA AND GIRAUT DE BORNELH
S' ie. us quier conseill, bell' ami' Alamanda   96
This is Need to Know, Pretty little A   97

AZALAIS DE PORCAIRAGES
Ar em al freg temps vengut 102
Now We Come to Our Winter Phase 103

CLARA D'ANDUZA
En greu esmai et en greu pessamen 106
The Dull Weight I Carry Inside 107

JOHAN DE PENNAS AND ANONYMOUS DOMNA
Un guerrier per alegrar 108
Because I'm happy, I'll Sing a Song 109

LOMBARDA AND BERNAUT ARNAUT
Lombards volgr' eu esser per na Lombarda 112
I'd like to be the L-Bard for L-Barda Girl 113

TIBORS DE SARENOM
Bels dous amics, ben vos posc en ven dir 116
I Can't Lie to You, Love 117

ISABELLA AND ELIAS CAIREL
N' Elias Cairel, de l' amor 118
Where's It Gone Elias C., Our Love 119

MARIA DE VENTADORN AND GUI D'USSEL
Gui d'Ussel, be.m pesa de vos 122
G., You Said Good-bye to All That Sings 123

ANONYMOUS
Dieus sal la terra e' l pais 126
God Wrote the Earth and Space 127

ANONYMOUS
No puesc mudra no digua mon vejaire 128
The Poets Who Wrote Our Book 129

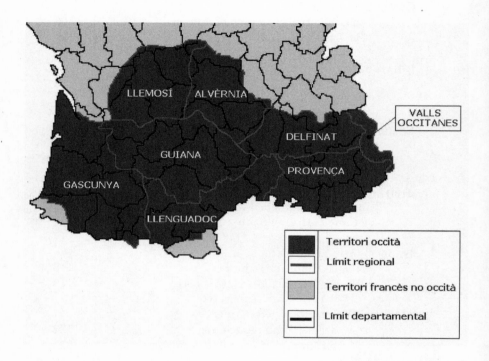

LLEMOSÍ ALVÈRNIA

VALLS OCCITANES

DELFINAT

GUIANA

PROVENÇA

GASCUNYA

LLENGUADOC

	Territori occità
	Límit regional
	Territori francès no occità
	Límit departamental

Províncies d'Occitània

Is You Is, Or is You Ain't My Baby? Finding the Trobairitz

It took me 20 years to start this translation. I needed the distance age brings to questions of love, I suppose, to begin. To translate the women troubadours, known as trobairitz, I knew I had to somehow gain access to their experience, which is believed to be the first sustained, cultural instance of women's writing. To start, I had to find a way to hear their voices, over and beyond the somewhat repetitive and stylized surfaces of the poems' conventions. Too, as women and poets, the trobairitz were intensely aware of their audience, all whom were members of the feudal courts to which they were bound by marriage, and so translating them involved understanding the complexities of the society in which they lived and wrote. Listening to the trobairitz's poems, I heard girls arguing with themselves, and with their lovers and their friends. Their poems argue for and mostly against the assumptions of what is called romantic love, the system of patronage by which they were bound. It is true that *fin'amor* was a notion of love invented by men involving chivalry to women in order to be better regarded by other, more powerful men; codes that continue still to influence representations of women's identity.[1]

So why translate the poems of 12th-century teenagers? There is something very moving about the drama and extremes of adolescence, a drama that is made melodramatic now by the film industry and television, even as much of the contemporary mind is still acting out *Romeo and Juliet*. Teenagers are comfortable with the extreme, which is good, because they are usually pretty powerless, despite the power of youth's attraction, to determine the way things go, even as our culture is obsessed with youth to the extent that many of us will die before we grow up. Popular music often plays to a sense of immediacy, of urgency, and often to a powerlessness regarding love, which is strongest when you're young. It helps to remember that childhood is an invention of the modern period, and that the teenagers writing these poems were women in their time,

---

[1] Romantic love is often called Courtly Love, a term invented by Gaston Paris in 1883 to refer to the troubadour's poetic system, which was invented in the unlikely atmosphere of the feudal court, where relationships were strictly prescribed.

which was not a particularly good time to be a woman. Women, in the eyes of the Catholic Church, were equal to men with respect to grace and salvation, but unequal in interpretations of the creation myth and original sin.[2] If a woman did not produce children she could be returned to her parents, or be put into a convent. The trobairitz's oeuvre speaks both to urgency and to the power of powerlessness, sometimes sarcastically, sometimes in anguish, and mostly opposing the fable of purity embedded in a poetic system derived by men. The poems also contain recognition of their unlikely power, which is the power of the constructed ideal, one continuously derived from the ongoing drama of women's history.

The troubadours who defined this code of chivalry called it *fin'amor*, or "fine love," wherein the troubadour pledges obedience to a woman of noble birth, paying homage to her in songs where the explicit reward is simply that he is "made better" by the exchange.[3] The trobairitz were, in fact, "the lady" of troubadour lore: 20 or so aristocratic teens, active from the mid-12th to the mid-13th centuries, who wrote poems which are the first recorded instance where "the lady" speaks back. The ingenuity of the troubadours cannot be overestimated. How better to secure a place in the feudal hierarchy than to invent a system of exchange that places the woman in ideal high regard? Scholarship in the latter half of the 20th century has established that courtly love was essentially "a system men created with the dreams of men," not women, in mind.[4] Their ingenuity cannot be reduced so simply, however, as we still have not sufficiently answered the question of how such poetry came to be.[5] That the troubadours created the unlikely tradition of *fin'amor* in a period

---

[2] William Paden, *The Voice of the Trobairitz* (Philadelphia, The University of Pennsylvania Press, 1998), 4.

[3] The terms of *fin'amor* share three distinct elements: love as a vehicle to spiritual betterment, humiliation of the troubadour before the lady, and an exclusive focus on married women of superior rank.

[4] Meg Bogin, *The Women Troubadours* (New York & London: W.W. Norton & Co, 1980). 57. Bogin speculates further on why only married women were the object of the troubadour's songs: "One of the early and persistent concepts of the troubadours was that the lady's love enhanced the *value* of her lover. Value (*valors*) was a vague concept which must have played on its double sense of spiritual and financial worth...According to the theory, both the lover and the lady had to have *valors*: she had it automatically through her husband, but the knight's could be increased, along with his *pretz* (merit), if he was a lover of a noble woman" (55). So the apparent love of the lady, in Bogin's view, is a win-win for the troubadour, bringing him both spiritual and financial value that he wouldn't have had otherwise.

[5] It's true that the adoration of the lady was prevalent in Arabic poetry. Occitania was a region at the crossroads of the ongoing effort of Christian crusaders to take Spain from Islam, and as many troubadours fought in the Crusades, they may very well have heard Arabic poems.

rampant with misogyny is remarkable in several ways. By associating an earthly woman with an ideal of purity, they were making a religion of love, which was tantamount to blasphemy. By turning their songs into performances that were sung by *joglars*, or actors at court, they were ensuring their economic reality. Borrowing in part from the Catholicism they openly despised, the lady in late troubadour poems was often read as a manifestation of the Virgin Mary, whose intrinsic purity cannot be tarnished, even by childbirth.[6]

Joglars

On the other hand, being "made better" by a beautiful woman can be expressed in vastly sexual terms, and often was in poems that are as equally ribald and profane as those apparently devoted to Mary. The lady would be chaste, yes, but what was the harm of insinuation if the situation was right? Their poems are full of *senhals*, or code names, an indirect

---

[6] Bogin, 50. Writing in the 1930s, C.S. Lewis maintained that religious hymns might just as easily borrowed from the troubadours' poems: "[T]here is no evidence that the quasi-religious tone of medieval love poetry has been transferred from the worship...of the virgin...it is just as likely that...certain hymns have been borrowed from love poetry." C.S. Lewis, *The Allegory of Love* (New York: Cambridge University Press, 2013), 10.

address that supposes the troubadours could be speaking to any woman in the room.[7] Thus, the provisioning of the sacred and profane is always in dialogue in the troubadours' system. Since women scholars in the last and present century have begun scholarship concerning the troubadour tradition, especially in regard to the trobairitz's resistant response to themselves as the idealized lady, the narrative of the phenomena has changed. C.S. Lewis, for one, saw the vassalage of the troubadours to the lady as a psycho-spiritual response of the unaccommodated, mostly unmarried, transient troubadour. Medieval marriages certainly had nothing to do with love and everything to do with matches of interest, i.e., the lady was of interest as a piece of property to her husband (if not a "sack of dung," which was a common epithet for women in the period). Pursuit of sexual pleasure was sacrosanct, as passion, or desire, was evil and a result of the Fall, even in marriage, where sex's function in the eyes of the Church was solely to produce progeny. The troubadours' *oeuvre* was therefore heretical because they placed *fin'amor* above all other duty. Instead of children, true love produces *joi*—which is what both love and the *poem* seek in the lexicon of courtly love.

So for many earlier scholars, the troubadours' elevation of the lady—over and against the utilitarian—was a social and spiritual rebellion, a "new feeling" that contained humility, courtesy, adultery, and the Religion of Love, i.e. romantic love, all in a period where none of these attributes were particularly manifest.[8] The troubadour is the uber rebel-heretic—poet(!)—humbly and courteously committing adultery with his lord's wife, in homage to a religion of love, which prior to this brief period in Occitan had not been seen before. I have always loved this narrative, because it aptly demonstrates the emergence of the new as both homage and rebellion. The voices of the trobairitz work the extremes of love embodied in the ideal of *fin'amor*, presenting a body of poetry that questions and critiques the basic assumptions of courtly love. Intensely aware of themselves as the subject, many of the trobairitz's poems debate the issues of purity associated with the Beloved in the troubadours' poetic oeuvre and raise questions of love, power, economics, religion, and political affiliation in gender relations. Even now as the Republican party continually strives to regain control of women's bodies in the US; in the sobering fact of women's poverty worldwide, and in the staggering

---

[7] Bogin, 50.
[8] Lewis, 10.

number of violent crimes against women everywhere, the trobairitz's powerfully defiant poems remind us that the *his* in history has been questioned for centuries.

THE GIRLS: BIO/GEO (GRAPHY)

Present day Montsegur

What is known regarding the lives of the trobairitz (first named so in the 13th-century Romance *Flamenca*) is found for the most part in the surviving biographies, called *razos*, or *vidas*, of the troubadours.[9] They were twenty or so young women from noble families in Occitan who wrote in *langue d'oc*.[10] We know some of their names: Tibors, Countess of Dia, Almucs de Castelnau, Iseut de Capio, Azalais de Porcairages, Maria de Ventadorn, Alamanda, Garsenda, Isabella, Lombarda, Castelloza, Clara d'Anduza, Bieris de Romans,

---

[9] Paden, 13. In the romance, the heroine trades secret messages with a knight who becomes her lover. At one point, the heroine's maid thinks of a perfect response, and our heroine thanks her as a *bona trobairis*, a good trobairitz. The word trobairitz combines the root of "trobar" which means both "to find" and "to compose" with the feminine suffix *airitz* and thus "a woman who composes."

[10] "[T]he language of yes (*oc*)." Reiger identifies a total of 43 (in Paden's "Some Recent Studies of Women," 104). Matilde Brucker cites 44. There were probably more, but there is no information remaining about others. My translation includes 26 trobairitz.

Guillelma de Rosers, Domna H., Alais, Iselda, and Carenza.[11] There are also many anonymously authored poems arguably written by women, some of which I include here. The known trobairitz lived in the regions where the Albigensians, also known as Cathars, would be slaughtered by order of Pope Innocent III less than 100 years later.[12] The rise of troubadour poetry and the spread of the Cathar religion flourished in Occitania from the middle 12th to the end of the 13th-century in the same regions and feudal courts.[13]

The ultimate repression of the Cathar heresy by the Catholic Church through the Albigensian Crusade was also the beginning of the end of the new poetry and the repression of Occitan or Provençal as a written language. To fathom what particular conditions made the trobairitz possible, it's necessary to look back briefly to see their emergence in the context of their times, in relation to Occitan's cultural and geographical uniqueness, and to the destruction of their language and country as a result of the Albigensian Crusade.

THE CODES OF JUSTINIAN AND THEODOSIAN

Compiled between 528 and 533, the code of Emperor Justinian limited a husband's right to his wife's dowry to *usufructs* (to "use" "fruit"), which means that he could use her land but couldn't claim it as his own or pass it on to his children. In a feudal culture where land, and the ability to

---

[11] According to Jenroy's "Liste par regions des troubadours dont la patrie est connue" (*Poésie lyrique* 1:321-25), the trobairitz lived in the following regions: Marie de Ventadorn, (Limousin, Marche); Almucs de Castelnou, Castelloza, Isuet de Capio (Auvergne, Velay, Gévaudan, Vivsrais); Comtessa de Dia (Dauphiné, Viennois, Valentinois); Garsenda de Forcalquier and Tibors (Provence); Azalais de Porcairagues, Clara d'Anduza, Gormond de Montpellier, and Lombarda (Languedoc). Reiger identifies a total of 43 (in Paden's "Some Recent Studies of Women," 104), Bruckner 34. The chronology of the trobairitz is hard to pinpoint, but it appears that they wrote from about 1173-1300. They emerged after the first period of troubadour writing, and disappeared during the last.

[12] Anne Brennon, "The Cathars in Occitan Society." In *The Voice of the Trobairitz: Perspectives on the Women Troubadours,* ed. William D. Paden. (Philadelphia: University of Pennsylvania, 1989), 87. Pilar Jiminez Sanchez's "The Origin and Spread of Catharism" suggests that "the origins of the Cathar heresy were the result of a [religious] construction which goes back more than 800 years." In *Le Royaume Oublie, La Croisade Contres Les Albigeois,* ed. Jordie Savall. (Bellaterra: España: Alia Vox, 2012), 81.

[13] Francesco Zambon's essay "Troubadours and Catharism" points out that the conjunction of the two phenomena led scholars to suggest that the "secret" or "coded" poetic system of the troubadours was an allegory for the Cathar heresy where "the lady, who is the object of the poet's love, represents the parish or diocese, the lover the Cathar Believer, and the jealous husband the Catholic of parish priest." In *Le Royaume Oublie, La Croisade Contres Les Albigeois,* ed. Jordie Savall (Bellaterra: España: Alia Vox, 2012), 92.

dispense and delegate it, was power, the limitation of a man's right to his wife's inheritance gave women their first chance to wield personal if not political power. Justinian also changed Roman law so that people of different classes (i.e. patricians and plebeians) could marry, which enabled him to marry Theodora, an actress and courtesan. Centuries later, Ezra Pound evokes Justinian in Canto CXVI, despairing of the power of the Lady or law to right the balance of power in human relations: "The vision of the Madonna / above the cigar butts / and over the portal…Justinian's / a tangle of works unfinished…."[14]

Theodosius, the Roman emperor who made Christianity a state religion, established the code that gave sons and unmarried daughters equal shares in their father's estate. The Theodosian Code of 394-395 arrived in Occitania by fiat of Visigoth invaders in the sixth century, and there is evidence in cartulary, a collection of legal acts, compiled in the 13th century by the Bishop of Limoges, that some women (40!) did act alone, or with their children, regarding property or other business.[15] While the number isn't staggering, it suggests that the easing of restrictive inheritance laws did open the way to the emergence of women's independence and, as heard in the songs of the trobairitz, to the emergence of female voices.

Contrary to established feudal principles in other regions of France and Europe, women in the *Pays d'oc* could inherit fiefs, as Eleanor inherited Aquitaine, and Marie of Montpellier inherited the city of her birth.[16] By the 10th century women controlled fiefs in the counties of Auvergne, Beziers, Carcassonne, Limousin, Montpellier, Nimes, Periford, and Toulouse.[17] In 1095, thousands of men answered the Pope's call to retake Jerusalem from the "Infidel."[18] With their husbands at religious wars, many wives of lords, primarily in Occitania, were left to run the courts. Trobairitz Almucs de Castelnau seems to have controlled Caseneuve during her husband's crusade. Guilhem de Poitou, the first troubadour, was in the East from 1101 to 1102, while Phillipia, his wife, governed Aquitaine.[19] Ever more recent studies of medieval women posit that women's position in the period was more complex than previously realized, and that

---

[14] Ezra Pound, *The Cantos* (New York: New Directions Publishing Corporation, 1943), 815.

[15] Paden, as quoted in Verdon, 10.

[16] Paden, 9.

[17] Bogin, 28.

[18] Bogin, 29. Four more Crusades would debut in the next hundred years.

[19] Claude Marks, *Pilgrims, Heretics and Lovers* (New York: Macmillan, 1975), 489.

the times were compelling scholastic and monastic observers to begin to recognize the moral potential of women's persuasion.[20] So far from Rome, Occitania was a region that was geographically influenced by Arab love poetry and the Jewish Gnosticism of the Kabbalah. Its borders were permeable in every direction, lying literally at the crossroads of varying religious and artistic influences.[21] This recognized openness must be why the Cathars were able to emerge so successfully in the Languedoc, holding meetings in barns, fields, and in the houses of their neighbors. Statements recorded by the Inquisition suggest that from the end of the 12th century, it was more often than not the nobility, led by women, who converted to Catharism.

THE ALBIGENSIAN CRUSADE

Though it is beyond question that the Cathars, troubadours, and trobairitz lived in the same regions and that the Cathar heresy and Courtly Love developed simultaneously in the 12th century, the historical relationship between the Cathars and the troubadours or trobairitz is still debated by scholars. The 20-year Albigensian Crusade (1209-1229) began when, under pressure from Pope Innocent III, Christian Europe took up arms against the Cathar heresy. When the French king Phillip II joined the effort, it became a war of land appropriation, since the pope had promised all crusaders that in addition to their sins being forgiven and debts paid, any land they conquered from the heretics was theirs to keep. The Occitanian Counts of Toulouse and Fox and the Viscounts Trevencal of Carcassone, Beziers, Albi, and Limousin, initially refused. Count Raymond of Toulouse, who openly supported the Cathars, was excommunicated and his lands put under interdiction.[22] He would be

---

[20] Paden, as quoted in Farmer, Duby, Herlihy, Stuard, and Bloch, 8.

[21] Manuel Forcano, "Occitania: Mirror of Al-Andalus and Refuge of Sepharad, " in *Le Royaume Oublie, La Croisade Contres Les Albigeois*, ed. Jordie Savall (Bellaterra: España: Alia Vox, 2012), 82. Forcano goes on to say "a fragile crucible which blended knowledge, music and poetry from learned and sophisticated Al-Andalus to the South, as well as France and Europe to the North, from Italy and the Balkans and the exotic world of Byzantium to the East...Occitania became one of the most active centers of Romanesque culture." (82)

[22] Denis de Rougement, *Love in the Western World* (Princeton, Princeton University Press, 1983), 84. Apparently Raymond did so only to assure that his land wasn't taken over by the Northern invaders, because it is clear from a letter of 1177 that he had no particular sympathy with the Cathars, though, or perhaps because, his mother was said to have been a convert: "The heresy has penetrated everywhere. It has sown discord in every family, dividing husband from wife, son from father, a man's wife from his mother. The churches are abandoned and

communicated and again excommunicated at least twice before his death in 1222. Within the next 20 years, the great Occitanian cities would be ruined. The crusaders seized Beziers, Carcassonne, Narbonne, and Toulouse—all. In Beziers, the crusaders demanded that Catholics hand over their Cathar neighbors. They refused, and the crusaders entered the city where, confused, they questioned Arnad Amalric, the papal legate, as to how they would know the Cathar from the Catholic. He replied: "Kill them all. God will recognize his own."[23] All were killed and the city burned to the ground. They continued to Carcassonne, where they cut the city's water supply. Raymond Roger Trencavel sought negotiations but was taken prisoner while under truce, and the city fell.

Cathars Leaving Carcassone

After the defeat of Carcassonne, Albi, Castelnaudary, Castres, Fanjeaux, Limoux, Lombers, and Montreal also fell. Though most of the actual Crusade lasted only months, the last portion of it was fought in and near Toulouse in 1128 where Count Raymond's son, also named Raymond, was unable to produce the manpower to rally, as crusaders laid waste to the countryside. Eventually, Queen Regent Blanche offered Raymond a treaty

falling into ruin…The most important people on my estate have been corrupted. The crowd has followed their example and has given up the Catholic faith, so that I no longer dare to undertake anything."

[23] Timothy 2:19: "The Lord knows who are his."

recognizing him as ruler of Toulouse in return for his fighting the Cathars and marrying his daughter to the child-king Louis, with the caveat that the city be inherited by the couple, and if they had no children, returned to the hands of the king. Raymond signed the treaty of Paris in 1129, and Toulouse was lost. The last outpost of Cathar resistance, Montsegur, fell in 1244, some 15 years after the end of the Albigensian Crusade.[24]

In the years that followed, French language and law were established in Occitania, and the marriages of Occitanian heiresses with Northern lords brought the largest fiefs under control.[25] The freedom that the Justinian and Theodosian codes had made possible vanished. Primogeniture was strictly enforced, so daughters no longer inherited land. Troubadour poetry was also a casualty of the Crusade. The Inquisition began in Toulouse, ostensibly to interrogate Cathars, but *fin'amor* came under scrutiny as well. Many troubadours went into exile in Spain and Italy, and those who remained stopped writing or sang of the Lady now turned into Mary, the virgin mother of Christ. The trobairitz and their poems were not heard of again after 1300.

GNOSIS/FIN'AMOR?

It may be historically impossible to prove that there are intersections in the means and methods of Cathar faith and the poetic system of the troubadours, but it's clear that the spiritual practice inscribed into the two are similar. Since Occitania was the target of the Albigensian Crusade because of its housing of heretics, it is entirely likely that there were as many troubadours that were Cathar as Catholic; and because noble women led the way in converting to Catharism, the Lady of their poems may very well have been Cathars, and trobairitz.[26] Both Catharism and *fin'amor*

---

[24] Adapted freely from the following sources: Sibly, W.A. and M.D., translators. *The History of the Albigensian Crusade: Peter of les Vaux-de-Cernay's Historia Albigensis.* Woodbridge: Boydell, 1978.
Eugène Martin-Chabot, editor and translator: *La Chanson de la Croisade Albigeoise éditée et traduite.* Paris: Les Belles Lettres.
Jean Duvernoy, editor. *Guillaume de Puylaurens, Chronique 1145-1275: Chronica magistri Guillelmi de Podio Laurentii.* Paris: 1976.
Sibly, W.A. and M.D, translators. *The Chronicle of William of Puylaurens: The Albigensian Crusade and its Aftermath.* Woodbridge: Boydell & Brewer, 2003.

[25] Bogin, 58.

[26] Rougement, 84. Piere Vidal, for example, in his poem "Thanks for Gracious Moments of Hospitality" lists the castles where he was made welcome: Fanjeaux, Laurac, Gaillac, Saissac,

called for secrecy; upon initiation, Cathars had to promise never to betray their faith, no matter what death awaited them, while troubadours and trobairitz were likewise sworn to secrecy in the terms of *fin'amor*. Like the troubadours, the Cathars praised chastity, without always practicing it.[27] Believing in the equality of men and women, Cathars were adamantly opposed to Catholicism and shared Courtly Love's antagonism of marriage. For the most part, they are thought to have been older people who had been married prior to their conversions, who believed that it was in their death *away* from this world wherein lay their salvation.[28]

The theme of death in troubadour poetry is likewise preferable to earthly rewards, *because* of *fin'amor*, a love that does not end. For Cathars, the true God existed in a world of eternal light beyond the warring, dark world of human existence. This dualism between light and dark is also performed in the *alba*, or dawn poems, but in the *alba* the dawn interferes with *fin'amor*, forcing the lovers to part as night turns to day, to return to the realm of human complicity and untruth. These *bons hommes chretiens* and *bonnes femmes chretiens* (good Christian men and women) pursued *gnosis*, or direct apprehension of God, within a defined structure. They chose their "level" of religious life from three classes: Listeners, Believers, and Perfect. The Listeners were people who didn't commit to the faith completely—a Listener was a kind of Easter and Christmas attendee, who, while friendly towards the faith, wasn't wholly of it. If Listeners chose to become Believers, they participated in the *cogenza*, a ceremony that formally bound them to the church. Comprising the majority of the movement, Believers were ordinary men and women who lived in the villages among their Catholic townsfolk, had jobs, didn't abstain from wine, eating meat, or sex; in other words, people who lived very much in the world of matter that their doctrine saw as fallen. Taught to be "in" the world, but not "of it," they followed the basic teachings of the Gospels: to love one another, to be faithful, and to seek God.[29] The Perfect became "perfect" wholly embracing all aspects

---

and Montreal, as well as the counties of Albigenses and Carcassa, all of which were well known houses and counties of the heresy. There are no doubt many other troubadour poems in the 2,500 of the period that could be read as Catharist. Rougement also suggests that when you see the word "true" before the words love, light, faith or church in troubadour poetry, it's a sign of Catharism. Someone other than I shall count the innumerable times "true" is used in the poems of the troubadours and trobairitz!

[27] Rougement, 85.

[28] Many people in the middle ages chose to spend the end of their lives in solitude and contemplation, often by entering either a monastery or convent.

[29] Sean Martin, *The Cathars* (Thunder Mouth Press, New York: 2004.), 52-59.

of the doctrine, thereafter taking the rite known as the *consolamentum*, usually on the deathbed, where he or she became the embodiment of the Holy Spirit, the living church itself. The *Kephalaia* of Mani describes how the elect person who has renounced the world receives the laying of hands, whereupon he is ordained in the Spirit of Light. As he approaches death, this spirit consoles him with a kiss, whereupon he venerates his own form of light, his anima, his *feminine savior* (emphasis mine).[30]

The troubadours' creation of *fin'amor* is likewise a seeking of "pure" love from a noble woman, unmediated by anything but the song sung to express it. The poems' methodology, rooted in *trobar*, begins newly each time, and belying *a priori* poetic structure, is arguably comparable to Cathar pursuit of *gnosis*. The poet who begins a poem created or "found" an improvisational method where the first stanza sets the terms of the rhyme, which the following stanzas can repeat in a number of ways.[31] The poem then records an origin that is quickly duty-bound in the exacting arms of *fin'amor* where it must conform to the behavior of Courtly Love. The subject of the love poem is fixed in the common scenarios of *fin'amor*—i.e. the modest poet/friend/lover pleads for love from the silent and snubbing lady and expresses his thwarted longing (which seems mostly to give him pleasure). If his song is successful in wooing his lady, he will be rewarded by the ultimate gift of *joi*, longed for and remembered in the experience of the song itself.[32] The troubadour can be reckoned as Believer who, through the fixed rhetoric of *fin'amor's* pursuit, receives joy (the ultimate consolation) and becomes Perfect.

Simone Weil, writing in the 1940s, finds further textual evidence of this connection in the second part of the "Song of the Crusade Against the Albigensians," an epic fragment, which dwells explicitly on the spirituality of the threatened civilization. She comments that the poet uses the same two words, *prix* and *paratge*, pride and courtesy, to mourn their loss, both of which became inestimable values in courtly love.[33][34] But what happens

---

[30] Cathar doctrine shares many affinities with Manichaeism, particularly in regard to viewing "consolation" as a sacrament given to the elect or "perfect" believer.

[31] Matilda Bruckner, Laurie Shepard, and Sarah White, *Songs of the Women Troubadours* (Routledge: New York and London, 2000), xvi.

[32] Bruckner, xvi.

[33] Simone Weil, *Selected Essays* (Oxford University Press: London, 1962), 39.

[34] When Weil's "A Medieval Epic Poem" appeared in *Cahiers du Sud* in 1943, it was understood that Guillema de Tudela had written the first half of "Song of the Albigensian" while an unknown poet had written the second half, which stands in distinct sympathy with the Cathars. Scholars

to the lady, to *fin'amor*, to *joi*, when it is the lady who sings? Allegory disappears. The songs of the trobairitz sing with varied emotions, always passionate, about the particular role of *fin'amor* and the ways in which the fictional ideality of the lady in the troubadour's lexicon places her in a precarious position, to her husband, to her lover, and to her self. Their poems nonetheless also express the ecstatic, often anguishing experience of *fin'amor*, which they place above all other feeling. The voluntary subordination of the troubadour to the lady in the pursuit of the essence of love, and the trobairitz's recasting of the pursuit from the receiver's perspective, is the beginning of the war between the sexes still being waged.

POEMS, THEIR TROPES AND AUDIENCE

Over and beyond the history with its inevitable lacunae and gaps are the poems, which are unlike any that came before or since. While the dynamic isn't complicated in the poems, it can get crowded! First, there is the Lady, the trobairitz herself, who speaks as girl and poet, who in dialog (debate) with her lover, whom she calls her friend (*amics*), understands herself both as an ideal and a commodity. Second, there is the lover, a man-boy, the troubadour, who wants to prove his love for the girl through his song, who mostly without mentioning it, and often despising it, needs to gain approval from her husband. Third, by mention or omission, there is the husband, the main audience, the feudal lord, to whom both trobairitz and troubadour are socially and financially bound, one by marriage, the other by vassalage. He is mentioned from time to time, always by the trobairitz, and usually as an oppressive force: part owner, part parent, part disapproving society itself, part failed lover. He is always regarded either through rebellion or in fear. Consider the following passage from the trobairitz Castelloza:

> My husband loves you more than I
> Because my songs make others soar.

now suggest that the second half of the poem was written by Gui de Cavahlon, a well-known troubadour, who fought against the crusaders in the Albigensian Crusade with Raymond VI of Toulouse. In what would clearly stand with Presentism theories of history today, Weil writes: "Today, whether as praise, or blame or excuse…it is willingly conceded that intolerance was inevitable in their days, as though inevitability varied with time and place. But every civilization, like every man, is offered the sum total of moral ideas and makes a choice.…If intolerance won the day it is because the swords of those who chose intolerance were victorious. It was a purely military decision" (37). She goes on to say that Europe never recovered the spiritual freedom which was lost as a result of this war.

My mother, father, all my kin,
They clap to see the pain I'm in.

And this, from an anonymously written *dansa*:

> So the green man bully,
> *He's the husband*
> Or beats and clubs me fully,
> *He's the husband...*
> He won't defeat me—
> I love just you or not;
> My heart is yours for free.
> *When the husband...*

The anonymous *dansa* elaborates the real danger of romantic love: the poet may put herself in danger, but she is defiant that her love be heard. Castelloza seems to understand her commodity value and to know that it is her songs—and the subsequent pain she feels in making them—which are valuable to her family. The poem also articulates her new, shameful understanding of her own participation in the fiction of *fin'amor*:

> I never loved or shared my trust,
> Until I saw it helped my fame.
> Since you were never real or true,
> I now spew these words on your name.

The poems' authenticity comes from an uncensored statement of their situation, as well as the poets' need for expression, no matter what may be the consequence. Fourth, there are the *lauenziers*, gossips, or spies, who are characters in the poems (and no doubt in the actual court as well) who disparage or plead the lover's case to the Lady (they are called "twisted sisters," "love killers," etc. in this translation). Sometimes the troubadours or trobairitz themselves play the role of spy or intermediary, as in this *tenso* between Alamanda and troubadour Guiraut de Bornelh:

> G., what you want, she doesn't care
> This is a game of give and take, so what you lose
> Just give it up and keep the show going...

The mediating presence of the *lauenziers* probably recreates the real tension in a feudal court, where *fin'amor* was a game that you could lose if your love was more than platonic. Finally, there is the poem, or the song, which is associated with love in the trobairitz poems. Castelloza again:

> I should give up on song,
> Since the more I sing
> The more love goes wrong,
> And these tears and groans
> Move in and build my home.
> My words leave me at risk,
> Yet even so I know,
> If I ended this poem right now,
> I've already droned on too long.

I can't get over how entirely their form of expression self-reflexively expresses the range of their desire. Meg Bogin and others have argued that the trobairitz wrote poems in the voices of "real people, and as earth bound...in a language unambiguous and personal," which is true, in so far as "real" people exist.[35] Of all the trobairitz, only Lombarda writes in *trobar clus*, the hermetic, "closed" style of some of the best Provençal poets, such as Arnaut Daniel. As mentioned earlier, I also believe that the trobairitz were very aware of the essential fictionality of their subjective position, which was foremost in my mind when structuring the sequence of poems in *Truth of My Songs*. While the art of *trobar* involves "finding" the measure, the measure is thus set and followed. Therefore, the poem, while always associated with love, is equally associated with itself, e.g. poem *qua* poem, which begins in the age of the troubadour, already to question the limits of language. In Maria de Ventadorn's *tenso* with Gui'd'Ussel, she worries about the rules of the song, now that Gui, a troubadour of great distinction, has given up writing:

> Gui, you said good-bye to all that sings...
> A question to make it clear:
> Does a girl state it man to man
> Or a man bow down to a girl
> And where's a book that maps that world?

---

[35] Bogin, 66-67.

As Lady Maria wants to believe in the rules, since in the pure terms of *fin'amor*, she has greatest power. In this instance, it's the troubadour who argues against the rules of *fin'amor*, having wearied of them:

> Maria, I gave the map to you
> And now in the ashes of my adieu,
> Here you are back to tune
> The old songs we crooned?
> No one's ever been on top,
> Woman, man, girl, and boy...

Scholars of troubadour poetry long speculated in the use of the word "friend" (*ami* or *amics*) in the poems. Were these poems really about platonic love?[36] Were they a pretense for an affair? We have seen how they impose religious allegory in the male troubadour's lexicon. Friendship itself is subversive in a feudal court, where relationships are set and rigorously controlled. This is acknowledged in the poems of the trobairitz as they question the assumptions of friendship offered by the troubadour, who after all isn't really in a position to offer it. Friendship appears to be something for which they longed, without really having the vocabulary for it. The *tenso* between Alais, Iselda, and Carenza gets close to a contemporary idea of friendship—two girls talking to an older, wiser girl about love in the abstract, what it's for, why they should want it, etc. Yet, there is the distance of rank that makes friendship impossible. Carenza is above the other two; she is an emblem of the matriarchy which mediates between the girls, their questions and wants, and their inevitable position as Lady, to which older women, bound by the tradition of *fin'amor*, also prescribe. In my translation, all three possibilities of friendship can, and do, apply. The poems of the trobairitz often address, either directly or indirectly or both together, the sometimes agonizing, sometimes liberating, sometimes ho-hum power of sexual desire.

---

[36] Gaston Paris's popular but ultimately disingenuous discussion of Courtly Love depicts the Lady who, in charge of the castle while her husband is on Crusade, is courted by troubadours who come to sing, in Paris's interpretation, platonically to her. The notion of the purity, or asexuality, of the encounter was one held for many years, until scholars couldn't ignore the eroticism of much troubadour expression. Many of the poems of the trobairitz, as well as those considered anonymously authored by women, consistently interrogated the troubadour about the nature of his love, in directly sexual and or argumentative terms.

ON TRANSLATION

I don't have a singular idea of translation, or examples of translations to single out as precedent for the liberties I take in *Truth of My Songs*, but I do have my "company," as Robert Creeley was fond of saying. I put Pound's translations of the troubadours, of Confucius and other Chinese poems in my corner years ago, as well as Louis Zukofsky's translations of Catullus and David Slavitt's translations of Virgil and of Dante's *Vita Nuova*. More recently, Pierre Joris's translations of Paul Celan's poems collected in *Threadsuns* have been a constant companion, as have been Donald Revell's rendition of Laforgue's work, Maxine Chernoff and Paul Hoover's translation of Hölderlin's later work, and Mani Rao's innovative version of the *Bhagavad Gita*. All of these translations circulate in the circumstances of the translator's own writing present, which is, like it or not, the only living place of reception. I agree with Pound in this regard:

> All ages are contemporaneous. It is B.C., let us
> say, in Morocco. The Middle Ages are
> in Russia. The future stirs already in the minds
> of a few.[37]

The trobairitz's concerns are still women's concerns, and to carry that across, I listened for contemporary sounds in which to make those concerns manifest. Lawrence Venutti's idea that the communication conveyed through translation is a troubled one seems accurate to me, as one would never set purposefully forward to mistranslate; and yet this is a claim made by philologists and linguists regarding most translated work that does anything more than transliterate the literal meaning of the original text.[38]

---

[37] Ezra Pound, *The Spirit of Romance* (New York: New Directions), 6.

[38] Lawrence Venutti, "Translation, Community, Utopia" in *Rethinking Translation: Discourse, Subjectivity, Ideology*, ed. Lawrence Venutti (London and New York: Routledge, 1992), 482. Venutti writes: "[T]ranslation never communicates in an untroubled fashion because the translator negotiates the linguistic and cultural differences of the foreign text by reducing them and supplying another set of differences, basically domestic, drawn from the receiving language and culture to enable the foreign to be received there. The foreign text, then, is not so much communicated as inscribed with domestic intelligibilities and interests." He goes on to question what formalist translator Gideon Toury called the "invariant," the element or elements that do not change, despite the translation of a text from one culture and language to another culture and language. The so-called "invariant" in the translation in *Truth of My Songs* is the communication of women in relation to themselves as subjects, which the history of ideas had generally heretofore ascribed as happening in a later period, prior to the discovery of the

I also love Derrida's insouciance (is there ever enough of it?) and would like to feel he is on my side in his address "What is 'Relevant Translation?'":[39]

> As for the word...I believe that I can that if I love
> the word, it is only in the body of its idiomatic
> singularity, that is, where a passion for
> translation comes to lick it as a flame or an
> amorous tongue might...and after having
> aroused or excited a desire for the idiom, for the
> unique body of the other...I don't know how, or
> in how many languages, you can translate the
> word *lecher* when you wish to say that one
> language licks another, like a flame or a caress.
> But I won't put off any longer saying
> "merci" to you, in a word, addressing this *mercy*
> to you in more than (and no longer) one
> language.

It's directly through the idiomatic transfer that *amor* revealed the singularity of each trobairitz, where her love (the armor in *amor*) via Derrida's caress was carried across to me. Both Ezra Pound and W.D. Snodgrass translated the music of the troubadours to the musical riffs of their period, and as I began translating these poems beginning in 2011, I heard the sound of 12th-century pop culture, a Middle Ages version of rap or hip-hop, the rebellious music of the young, whose love exists in a complex of concerns always personal, and yet indelibly set amid a society seen as oppressive, which is nonetheless the society whose influence on your always personal love affair, controls both its shape and outcome. As in rap, the poems are conversational, repetitive, angry, sad, or playful, and usually defiant to the system by which the singers feel controlled, which is both the poetic system of *fin'amor* as well as the feudal system in which they lived. Rap is an African American phenomenon, and it is also a world one, and I venture again into the contemporaneity of the ages to Livy, when he suggests that the second stage in the development of drama occurred in young Romans' burlesque of the "dignified dancing" of the Etruscans! The anonymous Mother Goose nursery rhymes dating back to the 14th century were also a subversive and proletarian critique—"when

---

trobairitz's oeuvre.

[39] Jacques Derrida, "What is Relevant Translation," in *Rethinking Translation: Discourse, Subjectivity, Ideology*, ed. Lawrence Venutti (London and New York: Routledge, 1992), 424.

Adam delved and Eve spun/Who was then a gentleman?"—which led to the Peasants' Revolt in 1381. "Doing the Dozens" was the mother of rap in this country, heard through the parlay of ex-slaves, though it crossed race and gender lines, sharing so-called common speech, an urban location, class consciousness, and a sense of itself as performance.

Truth of My Songs records the issues the troubadours and trobairitz were debating in present day idioms and speech patterns. The musical structures in my versions, as with rap or hip-hop, may be experienced better through listening to the musical variations of the dynamics and tropes of those mediums—incessant, sometimes annoying rhyme, thematic of bad and/or good love, in expressions of power within powerlessness—than by searching for the truth of their identities; identities, scholarship affirms, that are often impossible to verify. I would not presume to suggest that *Truth of My Songs* should replace Meg Bogin's or Sarah White's excellent transliterations of the trobairitz's corpus. Meg Bogin brought these women into the 20th century in English, and I am offering them to the 21st, so as to keep true to the terms of *trobar* as I have come to understand it. To that end, I have been faithful to the method, and as much as possible, to the music of the original, insofar as English can be faithful to an ancient Romance language. Before translating, I first read the Provençal, listening for a homophonic connection (most often I would translate the Provençal word to an equivalent sounding English word). To honor a vernacular that disappeared long ago, I worked to find approximate English idioms to lend the right tone for their constant one-upmanship. I freely change place names as well as the names of nobles, by omitting them or addressing them by their initials. Since the job of translator is to literally "carry across" an original text to another language, to another time, and in this case, a dramatically different period and culture, I restate many of the tropes in the trobairitz corpus in categorical terms in order to translate an oppressive power dynamic into contemporary terms. For example, here in a *canso* (a lyric poem in a single voice) by Azalais de Porcairages, the poem ends with an invocation to local power brokers, who she hopes will stand with her against her faithless lover:

> To God I commend Bel Elgar
> And the city of Orange
> And Gloriet and Caslar,
> And the Lords of Provence

I take these liberties to better foreground the timeless, tyrannical relationship of power to truth, since often in these poems, and in this poem in particular, the actual identity of an individual or place name is uncertain, lost, or defunct:

> I hand over the bank to God
> and the city of blank,
> all those prophets of buy and trade,
> the CEO's of all my days...

Additionally, I initialize the names of the lovers and other characters in the poems, to assist with syllable count and to intensify the need for secrecy. The translations circulate within the language of capital and commodity, as the relationship between the lovers involves an unequal economy, i.e. the troubadour who is often low born and in need of patronage, and thus in need of humiliation, and the lady who is noble, but in terms of *fin'amor*, dependent upon a knight's pledge. This unequal economy also applies to the trobairitz's frequent perception that the lover's idea of the Lady is a fiction. The poems perform different modes, primarily the *tenso*, or debate poems, in two voices, which dominate the trobairitz oeuvre. I compared Meg Bogin's 1976 *The Women Troubadours*, Matilda Bruckner's *Song of the Women Troubadours*, and Carol Nappholz's *Unsung Women: The Anonymous Female Voice in Troubadour Poetry*, which she had given me in manuscript when she was completing her PhD at the University of Denver in 1991, saying "make this into poetry..." While these scholars use different sources for their translations, there is not tremendous disagreement in their renditions. I include several poems whose authorship has no consensus. Alternately, I have chosen not to include others whose authorship does have such consensus. I did not include Gormond de Montpellier's *sirventes*, a pro-Catholic response to troubadour Guile Figueroa's poem attacking the Church. Her person and political affiliations differ vastly in tone from the other poems collected here, projecting a stance I couldn't affirm, and so couldn't translate fairly. The *sirventes* is a moralizing poem, political, personal or didactic in tone, which addresses subjects other than love, most often regarding social or religious authority, and *Truth of My Songs* contains two that are anonymously authored. The reader will also find several *tensos* where the known author is a troubadour, while the female voice remains anonymous. The *canso* is relatively rare in the trobairitz's canon—Countess of Dia, Castelloza, Clara d'Anduza, Bietris de Roman, and Azalais de Porcairages are known to have written them. Several anonymous poems included represent the canonical *alba*, or dawn poem, *balada*, and *dansas* poems. In essence, I translated the poems I liked, those that represented the range of trobairitz preoccupations, leaving out others that only repeated the tropes and maneuvers of the best poems in their canon. As in the originals, the titles of the poems are the first line. The music for only one of the trobairitz's poems has survived—*"A Chantar m'er de so que no volria,"* ("I Sing of Lies Better Left Unsaid") by Countess Dia, which is scored as follows:

CONCLUSIONS

I spent some time in the *Pays d'oc*, in Albi, with the primary intention of seeing the ruins of the Albigensian fortresses. They were closed. So, while there, I wandered into the city hall of the town, where hung an amazing painting called *Femmes des Albigenses*. It depicts a group of semi-naked women, all of whom would be killed that day or the next, confronting the crusaders. This willingness to live and die for a lived belief parallels certainly the clear pinnacle of *fin'amor*, where lover submits to the higher authority of the Lady, and Lady, if she hears the truth of his song, too gives way. The paradigm of obedience in Cathar culture came from a rooted belief that died with them: that order exists only when a feeling for authority, over and beyond its normative claims, is given freely without abasement, a desire that echoes through the trobairitz corpus. Their feeling was bound to *langue d'oc* itself. Simone Weil writes that after the Count of Toulouse had lost all his land and resources to the crusaders, the still-free city of Avignon submitted willingly to the vanquished Count, kneeling before him saying: "The whole of Avignon places itself in your domain—each of us renders to you his body and possessions."[40] The Count thanks then and says their *language* will be grateful for them for their action (emphasis mine)! It is a cause for wonder that the Roman church so feared the "church of love" (as the Cathar heresy is called in the annals of the Inquisition) that they came so far to slaughter them; but then, the messengers of truth to power often get the worst of it. In a comparable conundrum, the power the Lady holds in the tradition of *fin'amor* cannot be underestimated. The subject of the troubadour's song, the fine lady of noble origins, is referred to as *midons*, a man.[41] As subject, she has become man. As trobairitz, she is also a poet, and as *midons*, she is unequaled by any man, a knowledge the Countess of Dia displays, saying to her unfaithful lover: "But honey, you above all have the sense/To see that I am worth more than all the rest/Who makes poems better than we do?" The troubadour needs Dia's approval to play his role as poet in the court. Her marriage and her status as a poet makes her rank unquestionable.

In the end, to begin, I found that I had to forget to whom the trobairitz were singing, in order to hear what they were saying. In poetry, as I understand it, an audience is found in how poetry gives audience or makes things heard that could not be heard otherwise. I have listened to music of the Middle Ages, but I don't pretend to know what it sounded like to the people who lived then. We know that the troubadours' songs were monophonic and the monophony of the genre sounds somber to a modern ear, even while the text is ribald or full of *jouissance*. The troubadours and trobairitz, like the Cathars themselves, must have sensed that their language was under threat, both by the realities of the feudal system and the censor of the Church. I hear them singing their way to the gallows, like Brian in Monty Python's *Life of Brian*, but without the irony.

Of all language, the colloquial and idiomatic are the parts that change the most from one time to another, though through music and poetry, or the music in poetry, something—why not?—eternal continues. Obsolescence has never had a shorter window; and yet, the human dynamics of resistance and oppression remain remarkably similar, which may account for the phenomena of world rap, its place in the

---

[40] Weil, 40.

[41] Bruckner, xix.

recent revolutions in Egypt and elsewhere, the murder of Pashtun singer Ghazala Javed in Peshawar, and the incarceration of Pussy Riot for singing against Putin, etc. By giving audience, the past translated returns a song to be sung now.

—Claudia Keelan
Las Vegas, 2014

To my Sisters

And to my son Benjamin, whose life and music helped me to this work

ANONYMOUS

ALBA

En un vergier sotz fuella d' albespi
tenc la dompna son amic costa si,
tro la gayta crida que l' alba vi.
Oy Dios, oy Dieus, d' lalba! tan tost ve!

"Plagues a Dieu ja la nueitz non falhis,
ni' l mieus amicx lonc de mis no' s partis,
ni la gayta jorn ni alba no vis!
Oy Dieus, oy Dieus, de l' alba! tan tost ve!

Bel dous amicx, baizem nos, yeu e vos
aval els pratz, on chanto. ls auzellos
Tot o fassam en despieg del gilos,
Oy Dieus, oy Dieus, de l' alba! tan tost ve!

Bels dous amicx, fassam un joc novel
yns el iardi on chanton li auzel,
tro la gaita toque son caramelh.
Oy Dieus, oy Dieus, de l' alba! tan tost ve!

Per la doss' aura qu' es venguda de lay,
del mieu amic belh e cortes e gay,
del sieu alen ai begut un dous ray"
Oy Dieus, oy Dieus, de l' alba! tan tost ve!

La dompna es agradans e plazens,
per sa beutat la gardon mantas gens,
et a son cor en amar leyalmens.
Oy Dieus, oy Dieus, de l' alba! tan tost ve!

The alba *is a "dawn" song, a genre which performs the parting of lovers at dawn, amid bird song and flowers, while a watchman, who is playing a pipe, guards the lovers. The* alba *has also been associated with the Matins of Christianity, when God is asked to ward off the last dangers of the night. The Hawthorn tree plays prominently in the convention, operating as a symbol of fertitlity, and in the Christian tradition, as the cross where Christ was crucified. This* alba *is written from the woman's perspective.*

Under the green leaves of the thorn tree,
a girl holds a boy by her side;
and when the guard sees the sun rise,
oh God, uh-oh God, the night flies!

"Let what's Endless keep our dark alive,
and my guy for now by my side;
let the guard miss the sun's rise,
and God, oh God, slow the night's fly!

Beautiful friend, let's do it you and I,
down in the green where little birds sing,
though love is where they say we die;
and God, oh God! Swat the night's fly!

Beautiful boy, we'll play new games
down in the green where the little birds sing,
until the guard blows the whistle
and God, oh God, the night flies!

What air comes from there,
from my many manmade men?
I have drunk centuries of his breath"
and God, oh God, the night is day's fly!

The girl consents to her descent,
her face forever in their lens,
swears to love only you, the precedent—
and God, oh God, the night flies!

ALMUCS DE CASTELNAU AND ISEUT DE CAPIO

TENSO

Dompna n' Almucs, si. us plages
be. us volgra pregr d' aitan
que l' ira e. l mal talan
vos fezes tenir merces
de lui que sospir' e plaing,
e muor languent e. s complaing
e quier perdon humilmen;
be. us fatz per lui sagramen,
si tot li voletz fenir,
qu' el si gart meilz de faillir.

Dompna n' Iseus, s' ieu saubes
qu' el se pentis de l' engan
qu' el a fait vas mi tan gran,
ben fora dreich que n agues
merces; mas a mi no. s taing,
pos que del tort no s afraing
ni. s pentis del faillimen,
que n aja mais chauzimen;
mas si vos faitz lui pentir,
leu podretz mi convertir.

Almucs de Castelnau and Iseut de Capio were noblewomen and neighbors in towns in Provence, about thirty miles east of Avignon in the valley of the Lubéron. They were active from the late 12ᵗʰ and early 13ᵗʰ centuries. Almucs was the wife of Guigo de Castelnau de Randon, and is thought to have been a patron of troubadours. Iseut's origin is unknown, but her last name suggests that she was a member of a prominent family.

Girlfriend, I'm begging, don't be rude.
Drop this bad act and trade in your rage.
Forgive your low-down dude
and put on a good face.
Though he lies there dying,
he's sorry and keeps on trying.
If you want him dead,
at least let him take the last rites,
the showdown, and he will wake
to stop hurting you, and playing fake.

Girl, if he even seemed a little sad,
he might be able to erase
the upshot of his disgrace,
and I might pull back from being mad—
but I won't be dumb,
since he's gone deaf-mute, the bum,
and claims to regret his wrong: no release
for the liar who took away my peace.
Still, if you could make him come clean,
there might still be some love left in me.

CASTELLOZA

CANSO

1.

Ja de chantar non degr' aver talan,
quar on mais chan
e pietz me vai d' amor,
que plaing e plor
fan en mi lor estatge;
car en mala merce
ai mes mon cor e me,
e s' en breu no. m rete,
trop ai faich lonc badatge.

Ai bels amics, sivals un bel semblan
mi faitz enan
qu' ieu moira de dolor,
que. l amador
vos tenon per salvatge;
car joja non m' ave
de vos don no. m recre
d' amar per bona fe
totz temps ses cor volatge.

Mas ja vas vos non aurai cor truan
ni plen d' engan—
si tot vos m' ai pejor,
qu' a gran honor
m' o teing en mon coratge;
ans pens,quan mi sove
del ric pretz que. us mante,
e sai ben que. us cove
dompna d'aussor paratge.

Castelloza was a noblewoman from Auvergne and the wife of Turc de Mairona. There are different opinions regarding to whom this poem may be addressed. Some believe it is addressed to the trobairitz Almucs de Castelnau, others to Arman de Breon. It is possible that she was a habitué of the Court of Dalfin d'Alvernha, Count of Clermont (1155-1235).

1.

I should give up on song,
since the more I sing,
the more love goes wrong,
and these tears and groans
move in and build my home.
My words put me at risk,
yet even so I know
if I ended this poem right now,
I've already droned on too long.

My heartbreak epic, once before I die
please come and show me
your one, the only, face in history;
the other lovers swear
that you are a beast—
it may be right that no peace
will ever come from you,
but I was born to love forever,
and you're the one for whom I'm true.

I know I don't live up to your terms,
that my only gift is in feeling,
feelings that will never change
or turn toward another stranger.
Everything I trust
is all that I carry;
it's true we're not in the same class,
and the woman you marry,
will have her worth in hand.[42]

---

[42] As Castelloza is known to be a nobelwoman, it's probable that the rank she refers to here has everything to do with her lover's merit (*pretz*), which she regards as worthy of a higher station than her own.

Despois vos vi, ai fag vostre coman,
et anc per tan,
amics. no. us n' aic meillor;
que prejador
no. m mandetz ni messatge,
que ja.m viretz lo fre,
amics, non fassatz re:
car jois non mi soste,
ab pauc de dol non ratge.

Si pro i agues, be. us membri' en chantant
qu' aic vostre gan
qu' emblei ab gran temor;
pois aic paor
qui i aguessetz dampnatge
d' aicella que. us rete,
amics, per qu' ieu desse
lo tornei, car ben cre
qu' ieu non ai poderatge.

Dels cavalliers conosc que i fan lor dan,
quar ja prejan
dompnas plus qu' ellas lor,
qu' autra ricor
noi an ni seignoratge;
que pois dompna s' ave
d' amar prejar deu be
cavallier, s' en lui ve
proez' e vassalatge.

Dompna na Mieils, ancse
am so don mals mi ve,
car cel qui pretz mante
a vas mi cor volatge.

Bels Noms, ges no. m recre
de vos amar jasse,
car viu en bona fe,
bontatz e ferm coratge.

My words have got me nowhere,
nor has staying to see what letter you'd send,
what secrets whispered by one of your friends—
from the second I saw you I fell under
your spell, even now, here at the end.
And if, and when, you leave for good,
I'll feel less than I do now,
since joy has escaped the cage,
more hurt can't matter anyway.

I'd sing again, if it did any good
that I took your gloves—[43]
I stole them, shaking
even though I was afraid
you'd get caught
by the girl who loves you now.
I gave them back before she knew,
because at last I got the clue
that what I feel means nothing to you.

Others hurt themselves
loving those who don't love back—
it's a matter of power—
who has it and what marks its lack
isn't money and isn't class;
it's lost when you can't stop your mind—
I love whom I love and can't stop,
though it's my strength I've lost.

Oh sister A., I'm a fool[44]
who loves who is worst for me;
the one for whom I'd set down roots
is just the one with whom I shouldn't.

Mr. Man, my need for you
goes on and won't ever stop.
Through you I know that I'm kind,
and my belief props up this courage song.

---

[43] In the chivalric world, a glove was an important symbol for the hand that went to combat, which swore oaths of homage to the feudal fief. When Castelloza, the lady of higher rank, steals a glove from a knight, she upsets the status quo.

[44] In the Middle Ages, poems often had an *envoi*, or address, at the end. This *envoi* addresses *Dompna* na Mieils, a Lady Almucs and *Bel Noms*, or Good Name, apparently a *senhal*, or code name for the absent lover.

2.

Amics, s' ie. us trobes avinen,
humil e franc e de bona merce,
be. us amera, quan era m' en sove
que, us trob vas mi mal e fellon e tric;
e fauc chanssos per tal qu' ieu fass' auzir
vostre bon pretz, don ieu non puosc sofrir
que no. us fassa lauzar a tota gen,
on plus mi faitz mal et adiramen.

Jamais no. us tenrai per valen
ni. us amarai de bon core e de fe,
tro qu veirai si ja. m valria re
si. us mostrava cor fellon ni enic;
non farai ja, car non vuoill poscatz dir
qu' ieu anc vas vos agues cor de faillir,
qu' auriatz pois qualque razonamen,
s' ieu fazia vas vos nuill fallimen.

Ieu sai ben qu' a mi estai gen
si bei. s dizon tuich que mout descove
que dompna prei a cavallier de se
ni que. l teigna totz temps tan loc prezic;
mas cel qu' o ditz non sap ges ben chausir,
qu' ieu vuoill proar enans que. m lais morir
qu' el preiar ai un gran revenimen
quan prec cellui don ai greu pessamen.

Assatz es fols qui m' en repren
de vos amar, pois tan gen mi cove,
e cel qu' o ditz no sap cum s' es de me;
ni no. us vei ges aras si cum vos vic
quan me dissetz que non agues cossir
que calqu' ora poiri endenvenir
que n' auria enqueras jauzimen:
de sol lo dich n' ai ieu lo cor jauzen.

2.

If you'd shown just a little care,
shyness, truth or mercy,
I'd go with you anywhere;
you were mean and nasty, a thief,
but still I croon your name—
here, there, I don't care. It's my way
to sing to the ones I love,
no matter how they hurt or use me.

Until I saw it brought me fame,
I never loved or shared my trust.
Since you were never good or true,
I spew these words on your name.
I won't give you an easy way out,
admitting I burned you beyond doubt;
that's a trick you'd keep in store,
whenever you wanted to prove I was a whore.

I feel glad, proud even
when people say I sell my feeling
to anyone I happen to like,
or anyone who loves to talk;
let them say I'm not very smart—
I'll prove before I die,
I live to love and this is why,
I trick those who tell me lies.

Some say it's a shame to trade love for life,
but they are fools, since it gave me days of fun
to know when I saw you, you were the one.
But that's all gone,
my moment of faith—
you lied and told me not to worry,
because any day you'd come home,
and I'd have cause to live happily.

Tot' autr' amor teing a nien,
e sapchatz ben que mais jois no. m soste
mas lo vostre que m' alegr' e.m reve,
on mais en sent d' afan e de destric;
e.m cuig ades alegrar e jauzir
de vos, amics, qu' ieu non puosc convertir,
ni joi non ai, ni socors non aten,
mas sol aitan quan n'aurau en dormen.

Oimais non sai que. us mi presen
que cercat ai et ab mal et ab be
vostre dur cor, don lo mieus noi. s recre;
e no. us o man, qu' ieu mezeissa. us o dic:
que morai me, si no. m voletz jauzir
de qualque joi, e si. m laissatz morir,
faretz peccat, e serai n' en tormen,
e seretz ne blasmatz vilanamen

Now no other love is worth much;
joy is empty without your touch;
its trace turned my days to actual bliss,
days and days without pain just from your kiss.
I think I will always find happiness
in you, my absent boy: I can't change[45]
nor find joy, nor relief, from others,
except from the peace that comes to me in sleep.

I don't know why you're still in my mind
since I know you are both good and evil;
I still can't read your heart, stuck here in mine.
I won't send this: no, I'll talk and won't lie.
If you won't come, if you find you can't
say yes to me, or to our prize, I'll die.
If you let me die, you'll be the guilty man.
I'll be gone; my blood will stain your hands.

---

[45] Some manuscripts of the original show *convertir*, to change or convert here, while others
are emended to *convener*, a word used in judicial attribution meaning to call to justice, or to
summon. Is Castelloza continuing to affirm her love no matter the consequence, or is she calling
him to justice, or both? It's true that a call for judgment closes many *tensos*, and while this poem
is written in a single voice, the poet's recognition of her own merit or *pretz* in regard to the
absent lover is what calls forth her judgment upon him.

3.

Mout avetz faich long estatge,
amics, pois de mi. us partitz,
et es me greu salvatge,
quar me juretz e. m plevitz
que als jorns de vostra vida
non acsetz dompna mas me;
e si d' autra vos perte,
m' avetz morta e trahida,
qu' avi' en vos m' esperanssa
que m' amassetz ses doptanssa.

Bel amics de fin cortage
vos amei, pois m' abellitz,
e sai que faich ai follatge,
que plus m' en etz escaritz;
qu' anc non fis vas vos ganchida,
e si. m fasetz mal per be:
be. us am e non m' en recre,
mas tan m' a amors sazida
qu' ieu non cre que benananssa
puosc' aver ses vostr' amanssa.

Mout aurai mes mal ustage
a las autras amairitz,
qu' om sol trametre messatge
emotz triatz e chausitz:
e ieu tenc me per garida,
amics, a la mia fe,
quan vos prec q' aissi. m cove;
que. l plus pros n' es enriquida
s' a de vos qualqu' aondanssa
de baisar o d' acoindanssa.

Mal aj' ieu s' anc cor voltage
vos aic ni. us fui camjairitz,
ni drutz de negun paratge
per me non fo encobitz;
anz sui pensiv' e marrida
car de m' amor no. us sove,
e si de vos jois no. m ve,
tost me trabaretz fenida:
car per pauc de malananssa
mor dompna, s' om tot no. il lanssa.

3.

You stayed for days and nights
until I looked up and you were gone.
In your promise was your lie:
to love me all your life
and never say good-bye.
This is the worst thing you've done.
So now you love some other body.
"I" was extinct when I heard you'd left.
You, my faith, my hopeless gaud:
to love in sweet days lived without fraud.

Beautiful bastard, lover untrue,
I loved you because I love pleasure—
you left no clue to where you ride now.
I'm mute, lost beyond measure.
You paid in full, your awful for my good,
even though I tried never to cheat you.
Love shattered feels no shame—
it is a deadly mass that grows
and kills without remedy
until he comes here by his own will.

I'm not in the same category
as the other women in your life.
They hold truth close to their chest
hedging their bets to appear the best.[46]
But I've been glad to keep the faith,
to talk, not write, to you in the flesh.
It's clear that way, what I feel—
in this way rich girls grow even richer
each time you reach out your hand
and give to her what all girls need.

If I ever did you wrong
and sang to others or showed
just how I'd love another lover,
let every evil strike me down.
No, I sing this banal little song
because you've forgotten who I am.
I have to live and be this sad,
but I'd rather die, I'll say it again.
Please let me know what's in your head,
so I can decide to live or be dead.

---

[46] Since secrecy was central to *fin'amor*, Castelloza is violating it by her willingness to be seen talking to the absent lover. Her "richness" comes from her true expression, which is her honor.

Tot los maltraich e. l dampnatge
que per vos m' es escaritz
vos fai grazir mos linhatge
e sobre totz mos maritz;
e s' anc fetz vas me faillida,
perdon la. us per bona fe,
e prec que venhatz a me,
despois quez auretz auzida
ma chanson, que. us fatz fionsa:
sai trobetz bella semblansa.

My husband loves you more than I
because my songs make others soar.
My mother, father, all my kin,
they clap to see the pain I've borne.
All the wrong and all your fun,
it's all over, gone and done.
I'll never mention your many wrongs
if you'll just come back and talk to me.
If you hear the truth of my songs,
let me hold you in my arms before too long.

ANONYMOUS

BALADA

Coindeta sui, si cum n' ai greu cossire
per mon marit, quar ne l voil desire.

Q' eu be us dirai per qu son aisi drusa:
Coindeta sui...
quar pauca son, iuveneta e tosa,
Coindeta sui...
e degr' aver marit dunt fos ioiosa,
ab cui toz temps pogues iogar e rire
Coindeta sui...

Ia Deus no m sal, se ia n sui amorosa;
Coindeta sui...
de lui amar mia sui cubitosa,
Coindeta sui...
anz quant lo vie, ne son tant vergoignosa
q' eu prec la mort qe l venga tost aucire.
Coindeta sui...

Mais d' una ren m' en son ben acordad:
Coindeta sui...
se l meu amic m' a s' amor emendada,
Coindeta sui...
ve l bel esper a cui me son donanda;
plaing e sospir, qur ne l vei ne; remire.
Coindeta sui...

En aquest son faz coindeta balada,
Coindeta sui...
e prec a toz qe sia loing cantada
Coindeta sui...
e qe la chant tota domna ensegnada,
del meu amic q' eu tant am e desire.
Coindeta sui...

E dirai vos de qu m sui acordad:
Coindeta sui...
qu l meu amic m' a longament amada,
Coindeta sui...
ar li sera m' amor abandonada
e l bel esper, q' eu tant am e desire
Coindeta sui...

Nothing at all is known about the author of the poem. The balada accompanies a dance. It also sings about unhappy marriage, a frequent subject in the poetry.

I am so pretty
and I don't love my husband any more

This is why I'm loving
I'm pretty
Small and young and ready
I'm pretty
I want a husband who is gay
So we can dance the night away
I'm pretty

God help me if I ever really love
I'm pretty
Instead of this my false desire
I'm pretty
If he would finally die
I'd set my shame on fire
I'm pretty

There's one thing I know
I'm pretty
If my lover wanted me more
I'm pretty
My fine hope would make our lore
But he doesn't come for me
I'm pretty

There's another thing I know
I'm pretty
I'm the one he always adored
I'm pretty
But now I say goodbye to him
And any happiness he might bring
I'm pretty

With my song I dance a pretty dance
I'm pretty
For girls to sing here and far away
I'm pretty
Hope sings too without any chance
But I'll sing about my lover anyway
I'm pretty

ALAIS, ISELDA, AND CARENZA

TENSO

Na Carenza al bel cors avinen,
donatz conseil a nnos doas serors,
e car sabetz meils triar lo meilors,
conseillatz mi segon vostr' escien:
penrai marit a nostra conoissenza?
o starai mi pulcea? e si m' agensa,
que far filhos no cug que sia bos;
essems maritz mi par trop angoissos.

Na Carenza, penre marit m' agenza,
mas far enfantz cug qu'es grans penedenza,
que las tetinhas pendon aval jos
e. l ventrilhs es cargatz e enojos.

N' Alais i na Iselda, ensenhamen,
pretz e beltat, joven frescas colors
conosc qu' avetz, cortez' e valors
sobre totas las autras conoissen;
per qu' ie. us conseil per far bona semenza
penre marit Cornoat de Scienza,
en cui faretz fruit de filh glorios:
retengud' es pulcel' a qui l'espos.

N' Alais i na Iselda, sovinenza
ajatz de mi, i lumbra de ghirenza;
quant i seretz, prejatz lo glorios
qu' al departit mi retenga pres vos.

54

Though nothing is known regarding the women in this poem, some scholars have connected this tenso to troubadour Arnaut de Murehl, a troubadour active in the court of Count Raymond of Toulouse, a well-known Cathar locale. The names of the women have also been suggested to represent the three estates of women—Carenza the virgin, the noble Iselda, and the peasant Alais.

Lady C., your body is a form of light,
so shine now for two sisters, and please
tell us true from your wisdom,
since you know more than the rest;
should I go with that boy we all know,
or stay alone? That sounds ok to me,
for making babies doesn't serve much good,
and "wife" is a word for misery.

Lady C., part of me could love a man,
but birthing babies is not my plan;
your boobies fall and hang way down
and wives, they all wear frowns.

Lady A. and Sister I., you know
you're smart, still young, pretty and true,
more fresh in body and attitude
than the other girls in this neighborhood.
I'd say to you, if you want to have kids,
you need to marry a man like C. de S....[47]
and the fruit of your love will be sons:
wed to him, you're both pure and nun.

Sisters A. and I., remember me
in the last caring shadow you see.[48]
Pray to the splendor in the One,
though I'm gone, the me in you goes free.

---

[47] In Bogin's translation, the husband's name is Coronat de Scienza, possibly a Cathar name for Christ, whereby the initiate "crowned with knowledge" attains the state of pure gnosis wherin eternal life is achieved.

[48] Here Carenza speaks in the language of the *consolamentum*, the rite whereby Cathars became "Perfect," often in the moments before death.

ANONYMOUS

SIRVENTES (FRAGMENT)

Ab greu cossire
et ab greu marrimen
planh e sospire
e ab perilhos turmen,
can me remire
ab pauc lo cor non m fen
ni mos huels vire
que gart mos vestimens
que son ricx e onratz
et ab aur fi frezatz
e d' argen mealhatz,
ni regart ma corona,
lapolistil de Roma
volgra fezes cremar
qui nos fay desfrezar.

Sesta costuma ni sest establimen
non tenra gaire, c' an fag novelamen,
car lo rey Iacme no foron a prezen
ni lapostoli; c' absolva. i sagramen,
car nostres vestirs ricx
an nafratz e aunitz;
qi o tractet sia marritz,
per que cascuna entenda
que non port vel ni benda,
mais garlandas de flors
en estieu per amors.

Coras que vengua lo rey nostre senhor
que es semansa de pretz e de valor,
per merce. l prenda c' auia nostra clamor
de la offensa que fan sieu rendador,
que. ls vestirs an naffratz
e descendenatz
e desebotonatz;
per que nostras personas
ne van plus vergonhozas
prec que sian tornatz
per vos, franc rey ornatz.

This sirventes *protests the sumptuary laws that restricted rich dress. As such, it could well have been written by a noblewoman, the only women who had the right to dress as they pleased and who would have had the right to address King James I of Aragon. The poem may be influenced by another* sirventes *protesting the Treaty of Paris signed in 1229 that signaled the end of the political autonomy of Occitania.*

I grew coarse,
and I grew "marry man,"
plain and surprised,
I, perilous, trained men
to remix Me.
And when the heart grown fen
and my eyes see
the clothes, the bling
that constitutes Me,
I set the pictures on fire—
the judges and all
their laws, twinkling
upon history's pyre
that once dressed, undressed
and redressed Me.

All the customs and the ruling
will never last for long
for neither Prince nor Pope
could consent to that decree;
look at my dress!
What you think of as Me!
I'll see him in hell
who casts the world's veil
either me to hide or to sell.
Once in a circle of flowers,
naked in summer for love.

Chorus that comes with King
which is semen as it dribbles down,
pour mercy in our clamor
for the offense your evangelists do.
They make graves of our bodies,
buttons and chains clanged by consent,
by men, by women, by Status Quo,
its rabid congregation—
swallowing the dreck
they know is truth
from the virus your news anchors pass.

Senhors dauraires e los dauriveliers,
donas e donzelas que es de lur mestier
a l' apostoli mandem un messatgier
que escumenie cosselhs e cosselhiers;
e los fraires menors
en son en gran blasmors,
e los prezicadors,
e selh de penedensa
ne son en malvolensa
e li autre reglar
c' o solon prezicar.

Vai sireventesca, al non rey d' Arago
e a la papa que l sagramen perdo
car vilanesca an fag, si Dieus be. m do,
e ribaudesca nostre marit felo.

Ladies and Gentlemen,
send word to the men who power,
tell them our bodies
aren't to blame for the millennium
of shame brought in every hour
from the usual choir
who degrade Our names:
your preachers and your daddies,
and all the others who are afraid,
to stop the endless leakage
of those who speak this way.

Go, *sirventes*, to the White House,
to the UN, and exhume our bodies,
history of women, real and image,
while our husbands cowered in the shadows![49]

---

[49] Several more lines describing her clothes exist in the fragmented original, which I have omitted here.

RAIMBAUT D'AURENGA AND ANONYMOUS DOMNA

TENSO

Amics, en gran cossirier
sui per vos et en greu pena,
e del mal qu' ieu en suffier
non cre que vos sentatz guaire;
doncs, per que. us metetz amaire,
pus a me laissatz tot lo mal?
Quar abdui no. l partem equal?

Domna, amdui a tal meistier,
pus dos amics encandena,
que. l mal qu' an e l' alegrier
senta quecs a son vejaire;
qu' ieu pens, e non sui gubaire,
que la dura dolor coral
ai ieu tota a mon cabal.

Amics, s' acsezt un cartier
de la dolor que. m malmena,
be viratz mon encombrier;
mas no. us cal del mieu dan guaire,
que quan no m' en puesc estraire,
com que m' an, vos es cominal,
an me be o mal atretal.

Domna, quar ist lauzengier
que m' an tout sen e alena
son nostr' anguoissos guerrier,
lais m' en, non per talan vaire,
quar no. us sui pres, qu' ab lor braire
nos an bastit tal joc mortal
que non jauzem jauzen jornal.

Amics, nulh grat no. us refier
quar ja. l mieus dans vos refrena
de vezer me que. us enquier;
e si vos faitz plus guardaire
del mieu dan qu' ieu non vuelh faire,
be. us tenc per sobreplus lejal
que no son cilh de l' espital.

Poet and patron of poets, Raimbaut D'Aurenga, and possibly the trobairitz Comtessa de Dia, wrote this poem, as she was also a known participant in Raimbaut's poetic circle. This give and take circulates in the language of economics, as do other tensos between trobairitz and troubadour.

So *amigo*, I'm bankrupt,
my pain a debt
you don't pay and don't regret—
it costs too much, my wound, I bet.
You called me and I came,
I couldn't stand a sequel—
payback's a bitch that makes us equal.

Girl, love's a tall mister
whom two lovers share
so the good and the blister—
he's a little queer to each.
I've thought (and no shit)
that the durable dollar collars
me total to your cabal.

Dude, if you had a quarter
of my built-in dolor
there be virtue in my briar;
you call my pain your thwarter,
and my real locale calls you liar.
So I wear the happy mask, or the blue:
my expressions are all the same to you.

Girl, you bought those pictures from twisted sisters
who bash my rep and rap,
who sink you too until you're listing;
I can't come for you, but I'm still in your trap.
The twisted sisters keep on yapping,
you're at risk on this stage,
the sex is gone that once was our gauge.

Frére, you'll find no *merci* from me
since my pain clouds your eyes
from the me that calls to you for free;
you want to save me from lies
from idiots whose talk is toxic to me;
I'm a shrine you travel by
and you a dog, loyal, but chained to a tree.

Domna, ieu tem a sobrier
qu' aur perda, e vos arena,
que per dig de lauzengier
nostr' amors torne s' en caire;
per so deg tener en guaire
rop plus que vos, per San Marsal,
quar etz la res que mais me val.

Amics, tan vos sai leugier
en fait d' amarosa mena
qu' ieu cug que de cavalier
siaz devengutz camjaire;
e deg vos o be retraire,
quar be paretz que pessetz d' al,
pus del mieu pessamen no. us d' al.

Domna, jamais esparvier
non port, ni cas ab carena,
s' anc pus que. m detz joi entier
fui de nulh' autra enquistaire;
ni non sui aitals bauzaire—
mas per enveja. l deslial
m' o alevon e. m fan venal.

Amics, creirai vos per aital
qu' aissi. us aja totz temps leial.

Domna, aissi m' auretz lejal:
que jamais non pensarai d' al.

Yeah, well now I've almost gone bust,
set to lose cash and amour, our alchemy,
twisted sisters staking misery,
making dumpy ruins of our lust;
I'd spot you before you know you're found,
better than a cop, a saint,[50] a stalker,
you're my one, I'm your streetwalker.

Dude, I know you make all girls
baggage, target, and/or shrine,
though you front a different line
with bros who call us pearls.
No matter how close you keep me in sight,
there are other marks there too.
You can't know my dreams at night—
I can't shatter if your aim is true.

Trick, I will never again shoot my piece,[51]
or ride with my posse,
if since we got raunchy
I signed another lease.
I'm not a con;
but the twisted sisters give no peace,
until their lies prove me a cheat.

Boy, no choice but to catch your cred,
that no one else will make our bed.

Darlin', my cred is in our bed,
there's no one else inside my head.

---

[50] The original Provençal refers to a Saint Martial, who was the patron saint of Limousin, and appears elsewhere in troubadour poetry. Nothing else is known about him.

[51] To "shoot your piece" evolves from to "make your peace." Raimbaut d'Aurenga is associating his love for his lady to the valors of war and comradeship, two inestimable values in courtly love (and rap). It is also a pun for the poem, i.e. he will never make another song and never have any other friends if he has in fact cheated upon his lady. "Con" or "the rule of Con" in Provençal is a euphemism for female genitalia.

RAIMON DE LA SALAS AND ANONYMOUS DOMNA

TENSO

[Raimon]

Si. m. fors graziz mos chanz, eu m' esforcera
e dera. m gauz e deporz e solaz,
mas aissi m sui a non chaler gitaz
que ma domna, que a toz iorz esmera,
co qu' eu li dic, non deigna en grat tener,
qu' apenas sai entre, Is pros remaner
ni non sui ges cel qe era antan
aissi me volf mos covinenz e. Is fran.

Ha las! cum muor quant mi membra cum era
gais e ioves, alegres, envesaz,
e quant m' albir qu' eu sui de ioi loignaz,
per pauc mos cors del tot no. s desespera.
E dunc mei hueill, cum la pogron vezer?
Car n' ai perdut d' els e de mi poder;
ço m' an ill faz, don mos cors vai ploran,
qu' eu non puos far conort nib el semblan.

Ha! bella domn' aras cum be. m semblera
que, on que fos, degues humilitaz
venir en vos que tant humil semblaz
vers mi, que ia a mos iorz no. s camgera.
Amors n' a tort, que. us fai dur cor aver
e vos sabez, qar l' en donza poder,
qar si amors e vos es a mon dan,
las! ges longas non ouos soffrir l' afan.

This exchange is between Raimon de la Salas, who is thought to have served in the court of Hugh II of Baux, Viscount of Marseilles, and an unnamed lady.

If I could feel some gratitude I'd sing
and croon tunes, measure pleasure, peace.
But I was janked, my feelings fleeced
because my girl, swag-lit-lady-thing,
shut her open doors to what I say,
and now I can't see my friends by day.
No, a what-was-me sank into the used-to-be,
cray girl so twist, so broke, my "know" ran free.

Ugh, my-first-me dies in the mind.
He was blithe, up-pup his pet toy,
and here I live so far off from joy,
my heart now finds nothing kind.
So how can I open my eyes to look at her,
when I can't find my own sight, or my others?
My eyes and me did this we cry,
ease and rest, flew with the me who died.

Oh girl, it's true now what I know,
that wherever you're lost or hid, Jen[52]
could find you, and help our love mend,
her eyes true-lit in its sweet glow.
Love is wrong hid hard in a tower;
you taught me so, giving love that power.
If both Love and you want to do me in,
this pain will destroy me and win.

---

[52] Humility (*humilitaz*) in the troubadour's lexis is close to what Confusicianism calls "Jen," which is human-heartedness; goodness, benevolence, man-to-man-ness; what makes man distinctively human or that which gives human beings their humanity. Seeing "Jen," the lovers may see their own redemption. Here Raimon appeals to the unknown lady to find her humility (called "Jen" here) so the lovers may see their own redemption. In an etymological caress of which Derrida might approve, Jen in English comes from Guinevere, meaning "white enchantress," another form of the feminine divine.

[Domna]

Bel dolz amics, ia de mi no. s. clamera
vostre bel cors cortes et enseignaz,
si saubessez qals es ma voluntaz
ves vos, de cui sui meilz hoi q' er non era,
e non creaz qu' e. us met' en non chaler
car gauz entier non puesc senz vos aver
a cui m' autrei leialmen senz engan
e. us lais mon cor en gauge on qu' eu m' an.

Mas una genz enoiosa e fera
cui gauz ni bes ni alegrers non plaz
nos guerreian, don mos cors es iraz,
car pen ren als senes vos non estera.
Pero en mi avez tant de poder
q' ab vos venrai quant me. I farez saber
mal grat de cels q' enqueron nostre dan
e. pesa. m fort car senz vos estauc tan.

Don't say such things to me, fine man.
Your used-to-be would see I'm not to blame
since he could still read my desire's name;
today again it's you, more than I planned.
I don't do jank, and no one's feelings fleeced;
there's no *joi* without you, no *ahh*, no release.
In my joy is trust, not deception,
My love stays when I go, no defection.

But savage folk, the gossips and spies,
diss on what's happy or sweet or sage,
make war on our love, fires my heart to rage;
I haven't come to guard us from their lies;
it's you who holds the power.
Say the word, and I'll be there in an hour.
In spite of all who want to see us pay,
it kills me to stay so long away.

ANONYMOUS

DANSA

Quan vei los praz verdesir
e pareis la flors granada,
adoncas pens e consit
d' amors qu' aissi m' a lograda,
per un pauc non m' a tuada.
Tan soven sospir
d' anc non vi tan fort colada
senes colp ferir.   *Aei!*

Tota noit sospir e' m pes
e tressalh tot' endormida,
per oc car veiaire m' esperan
que' l meus amics se ressida.
A Deus, com serai garida
s' aissi devenegues,
un noit per escarida
qu' a me s' en vengues!   *Aei!*

Domna qui amors aten
ben deu aver fin cortage.
Tai n' i a qu'ades la pren,
pois la laissa per folatge:
mas eu l
en tenh fin coratge
aissi leialmen
qu' ance domna d' al meiu paratge
non o fetz tan gen.   *Aei!*

Domna qui amic non a,
ben si gart que mais non aia,
qu' amors ponh oi e dema
ni tan ni quan non s' apaia:
senes colp fai mort e plaia.
Ja non garira
per nul metge qu' el e aia,
s' amors non lo' i da.   *Aei!*

Nothing is known about the author of this poem.

When I see the fields go green
and the red flowers sprout,
I begin again to feel
the bad love we were about,
yes, the fiction where we mostly killed me.
Today I know and wonder why
I never saw that blow coming,
a blow never struck and even still I died.   *Ay!*

All night now I *hmm* and fret
and shudder in my sleep,
since I wait and won't regret
my guy waking to our keep.
Dear God, if he will come to me
even one night by chance,
should dark or luck let me free,
I'll wake up from this trance.   *Ay!*

Girls loving boys are liberal,
making love with any or all—
boys who think they touch her solely
call her crazy as she falls:
but in him my aim was lethal
it was for real
and so I left my people
because of love and zeal.   *Ay!*

Sister without a lover
has sister love, self-rule,
and the snake in time finds cover,
his *gimme* never full.
He kills or hurts without aim.
Our girl won't find a cure
from quack or shrink or more of the same,
until she dies and night spells her name.   *Ay!*

Messagier, levaz mati
e vai m' en la gran jornada,
la chancon a mon ami
li portatz en sa contrada:
digas li que mout m' agrada
quan membres del son
qu' el mi ditz quan m' ac baizada
soz mon paveillom.   *Aei!*

Dins ma chambr' encortinada
fon el a lairon;
dins ma chambra ben daurada
fon el en preison.   *Aei!*

Go when the sun rises,
go from me for a day's drive.
Sing this to Mr. Make-Me-Die
in his home where he hides.
Tell him I'm in bliss
when I sing the tune
he sang to me when we kissed
under cover in my room.   *Ay!*

My room hung with tapestries
where he lay and hid;
in my posh room,
prison for what we did.[53]   *Ay!*

---

[53] This poem is unusual in the trobairitz corpus, which includes only one other that evokes spring in this manner. The anonymous lady expresses a curious shame, different in kind from the humiliation experienced in *fin'amor*, that troubadour poems conventionally express. The last stanza employs a traditional *tornado* (return) or *envoi*, seen in several of the poems here, which hands off the poem, so to speak, to a messenger, who takes the poem to the beloved.

GUILLELMA DE ROSERS AND LANFRANCS CIGALA

TENSO

"Na Guillelma, man cavalier arratge
anan de nuieg, per mal temps que fasia,
si plagnian d' alberc en lor lengatge;
auziron o dui, qui per drudaria
s' en anavan vers lur domnas non len;
l' us s' en tornet per servir cella gen,
l' autres anet vers sa domna corren;
quals d' aquels dos fes miels so que. l tagnia?

Amics Lanfrancs, miels complit son viatge,
al meu semblan, cel que tenc vers s' amia;
e l' autres fes ben, mas son fin coratge
non poc saber tan ben sidonz a tria
com cil que. l vi denansos oils presen,
qu'atendut l' ac sos cavalliers conven:
e val trop mais qui so que dis aten
que qui en als son coratge cambia.

Domna, si us platz, tot quan fes d' agradarge
lo cavalliers que par sa gaillardia
garda. ls autres de mort e de damnage
li moc d' amor; que ges de cortezia
non a nuls oms, si d' amor no. l deisen:
per que sidons deu. l grazir per un cen,
car deslivret per s' amor de turmen
tanz cavaliers, que se vista l' avia.

Lanfrancs, jamais non razonetz musatge
tan gran quan fon d' aicel qu' aisso fasia,
quar sapchatz ben, mout i fes gran oltratge;
pois bels servirs tan de cor li movia,
car non servi sidons premieiramen?
Et agra 'n grat d' ell' e dels eissamen,
pois per s' amor pogra servir soven
en mans bos locs, que faillir noi podia.

Lanfranc Cigala was from a prominent Genoese family, who served as a judge and public servant. Guillelma, who is thought to have been a noblewoman of Provence, may have exchanged this tenso with Lanfranc when he served as Genoese ambassador in 1241.

"It was a cold and stormy night
when some sad strangers, talking in the dark,
wished aloud for a place dry, and free of danger.
Two lovers going to their girls heard them.
While one ran back to offer cover,
the other ran on to the mating game:
What would you do if you were a lover?[54]

The way I see it love's all about trust
those who make their own beds do best;
who cares that he gave help to strangers?
All she saw was he'd flunked the test.
While her sister held her man in her arms,
she lay alone, afraid he was harmed.
I'd choose him who come homes to me,
and drop the one with Jesus syndrome.

You shouldn't even use the word trust,
since it was belief in love that showed him
how to help the rest escape harm or death.
That's the test—to love who most needs love.
She should fall on her knees and see
with open eyes that this man who loves her
who stopped to aid the lost, the hungry, the cold—
He did what only great hearts are told.

So now you're down to justify
a guy who lives to rectify—
His code has zero to do with love;
if his act meant to exemplify,
why so late to her above all?
All of them would've been grateful—
There's no lack of down and outs
to help, in places closer to home.

---

[54] Written after the Albigensian Crusade, the strangers referred to here may be Cathars who survived. The troubadour expresses a Christian love that is non-discriminating. Guilielma expresses a feeling that promotes no other devotion outside the dictates of a seemingly secularized *fin'amor*. She believes it is the knight's duty to serve her, a noblewoman, first.

Merce vos quier, domna, s' ieu dic follatge;
qu' oimais vei so que tot o mescrezia:
que non vos plai qu' autre pelegrinatge
fassen li drut mas vers vos tota via;
pero cavals qu' om vol que biort gen
deu om menar ab mesur' et ab sen,
e car los drutz cochatz tan malamen,
lur faill poders, don vos sobra feunia.

Ancar vos dic que son malvatz usatge
degra laissar en aquel mezeis dia
li cavalliers, pois domna d' aut paratge
bella e pros dec aver en baillia;
qu' en en son alberc servion largamen,
ja el no. I fos; mas chascuns razon pren,
quar el sis en tan de recrezemen
qu' al major ops poders li falliria.

Domna, poder ai ieu et ardimen,
non contra vos que venses en jazen,
per qu' ieu fui fols car ab vos pris conten,
mas vencut voill que m' ajatz, com que sia.

Lanfrancs, aitan vos autrei e. us consen
que tan mi sent de cor e d' ardimen
qu' ab aital geing com domna si defen
mi defendrial plus ardit que sia."

Well excuse me, lady, I'm a simp.
What I knew all along is true:
your happiness will always elude
any way but that which leads to you.
If you want to teach a horse to jump,
you guide it with brains, and become sage.
Lovers go lame when spurred too hard.
His limp is your due, and now you rage.

This is the last time I'll say it—
that man should do what's fit
right now and pay his dues
to his fine and beautiful woman.
When she's at home the feast begins,
even when he's gone; but he's chicken.
Everyman's a hero, but that wimp,
if real bad showed up, he'd fly the coop.

Lady, I'm strong and I'm firm
(—not for you, I could have you in my sleep,
the second time won't come so cheap).
Do what you can to best my rhyme.

Head's up, here's a promise I won't break:
with everything I know and all I feel,
with all my brains for my own defense,
I'll elude the words of any men."

GARSENDA AND GUI DE CAVAILLON

TENSO

Vos que. m semblatz dels corals amadors,
ja non volgra que fossetz tan doptanz;
e platz me molt quar vos destreing m' amors,
qu' atressi sui eu per vos malaanz.
Ez avetz dan en vostre vulpillatge
quar no. us ausatz de preiar enardir,
e faitz a vos ez a mi gran dampnatge;
que ges dompna non ausa descobrir
tot so qu' il vol per paor de faillir.

Bona dompna, vostr' onrada valors
mi fai temeros estar, tan es granz,
e no. m o tol negun' autra paors
qu' eu non vos prec; que. us volria enanz
tan gen servir que non fezes oltrage—
qu' aissi. m sai eu de preiar enardir—
e volria que. I faich fosson messatge,
e presessetz en loc de precs servir;
qu' us honratz faitz deu be valer un dir.

"The Comtessa de Proensa" Garsenda de Forcalquier *was one of the most powerful women in Occitanian history. In 1193, her grandfather William de Forcalquier signed the treaty of Ais, so that Garsenda, then 13, would inherit Forcalzuier, and marry Alfonso, Count of Provence. When Alfonso died, she became regent of Provence, where she was the focus of troubadours, among them Gui de Cavallier, who was rumored to be her lover. Garsenda died in 1257.*

You so blubber in my luver junk,
so don't go so slow to my nose worth.
Then you'll flubber in the grassy cover,
because I'm *phew* with snotty hurt.
You dead bunny in the long run,
if you blob the talk of our dovey case;
and *ouch ow ow* for two you so refuse,
while lady junk floats in outer space:
Mr. Mute throw dirty over our two-face.

Your upper town-town skanks my stutter,
your stanky rank-rank burns my butter;
smug in the stats choking my home-speech.
Suss it served up, pup-pup like a brother—
no chow use for abuse to my luck lover,
(see, I *do* lob talk of the bird case).
If only my lonely might message you,
you make big halo through sex's place,
my lonely stats my mouth, my stake space.[55]

---

[55] Garsenda is speaking in the first *cobla*, or stanza, and Gui responds in the second. My Garsenda speaks girlesque and Gui is responding to the insult of the first stanza, where she has essentially told him in that he is "too hesitant," i.e. won't force the moment to its crisis, or have sex. He is offended that he is playing at the *fin'amor* game, and responds with a disparaging of both her rank and her sex, i.e. the "stanky." Then he also insults his own song because he "susses" or understands that the poem has become a domestic animal, a dog with no bite, a "friendly" brother. His anger relents and the poem ends with his hope that his words reach her heart.

GUILLEM RAINOL D'AT AND ANONYMOUS DOMNA

TENSO

Quant aug chantar lo gal sus en l' erbos
e' l pic e' l iai e' l merl' e' l coaros
e' l rossignol e l' aguisat perier,
farai un vers ses prec e ses somos.
Ma domn' es tan bell' e cortes' e pros
que' m fai loirar plus que falcos lanier.

Seingner, tan m' es mals e contrarios,
cent ves ai cor que mi parta de vos,
mais anc non vi home tan plasentier.
Mas d' una ren est ben aventuros:
qant sent venir esterlins orgoillos,
ades m' escont en granj' o en sellier.

Domna, tostemps vos ai mon cor cellat:
per qu n' avez de mi lauzor e grat
quant non amest cusson ni fatonier,
anza lo fugist om eu tornei rengat
qu' anc no' i fos pois, pos m' o agues vedat.
Mais am flauzons e sopas en sabrier.

Seigner, tostemps vos aurei prezicat
que vendessem so maior porc faissat
e vestissem Miquel, so berbeguier;
fezessem li blizaut fendut trepat
—tant a gen cors e bella maiestat,
cent vez er pres e lei de cavallier.

Domna, Miquels volria fos pendutz,
que tant l' anas qu' en son oer fols tengutz,
lo bacalar trachor mensoneguier.
Que ar vos ius encontra sas vertutz
que ia Miquels ni sos avers lanutz
non estara ab vos un an entier.

Seinger, cals es aicel c' om a tondutz
—uns grans, uns loncs, ab esperos agutz,
entopenatz a lei de cavallier?
Tant me mandet amistatz e salutz
e'm graziz mais que si fos bous cournutz,
car dei un pol a son tersol lanier.

Guillem Rainol D'At was a minor Provençal troubadour from Apt in the Vaucluse. He witnessed documents in Garsenda's court in 1209. This poem, along with other lighthearted tensos, was apparently written with his wife.

When I hear the cock crow in the parks,
pecker, jay, blackbird, the redstart,
nightingale and the greenfinch,
I write a short song no one asks for or wants.
My lady is fine and civil, my habit.
She pulls me more than a wooly hawk.

Boy, you are too bad too rude.
I almost flew one hundred times,
but I never heard a boy use words like you.
Just to show how you are a lucky dude,
when I see Mr. Lively "money-man" near,
I go and hide inside the barn or cellar.

Girl, I hide my heart from view,
for that I give credit to you.
You'd never love a bum or fool.
No, you'd ditch them like I did war;
never fought there again, since you forbade me.
Now I eat cheese pastries, and bread with gravy.

You know I begged and begged
to sell our best striped skins
to dress Miguel, my toy boy.
Let's deck him in torn clothes—
with that hot body and attitude,
he's the man to rule the roost.

I'll watch your boy Miguel hang,
since loving him makes me your *thang*;
that dodgy liar, young piece of trash.
I swear to you by his cheap ass,
neither Miguel nor his sheepy stash
will get near to you on any day.

Baby, who is that bald one,
huge, tall, with nice sharp spurs,
decked out like he's the one for sure?
He friends me with so many likes,
a horned bull couldn't post more sweet words;
so now I'm chicken for his woolly bird.

ANONYMOUS

BALADA

Quant lo gilos er fora,
bel ami
vene-vos a mi.
Balada cointa e gaia
quant lo gilos er fora...
faz, cui pes ne cui plaia,
quant lo gilos...
pel dolz can qe m' apaia,
qe' us audi
seir e de maatin.
quant lo gilos...
Amic, s' eu vos tenia
quant lo gilos...
dinz ma chambre garnia,
quant lo gilos...
de ioi vos baisaria,
qar n' audi
ben dir l' autre di.
quant lo gilos...
Se' l gilos mi menaza
quant lo gilos...
de baston ni de maca,
quant lo gilos...
del batra si se' l faza,
qe' us afi,
mon cor n' s cambi.
quant lo gilos...

Nothing is known about the author of this poem.

When the husband is away,
beautiful boy,
come to me
A dance, a groove, so sweet
when the husband is away
I play to you for free
when the husband...
Singing notes complete
you first sang to me
one night into the day
when the husband...
Love, if you I find
when the husband
in the room made with you in mind
when the husband...
we'll do more than kiss
since I could freely die
in your words the other day
when the husband...
So the green man bully
he's the husband
or beats and clubs me fully
he's the husband...
he won't defeat me;
I love just you or not
my heart is yours for free
when the husband...

COMTESSA OR BEATRIZ DE DIA

CANSÒ

1.

Ab joi et ab joven m' apais,
e jois e jovens m' apaia,
que mos amics es lo plus gais,
per qu' ieu sui coindet' e guaia;
e pois ieu li sui veraia,
bei. s taing qu' el me sia verais;
qu' anc de lui amar non m' estrais,
ni al cor que m' en estraia.

Mout mi plai, quar said que val mais
cel qu' ieu plus desir que m' aia,
e cel que primiers lo m' atrais
Dieu prec que gran joi l' atraia.
e qui que mal l' en retraia,
no. l creza, fors cel qui retrais
c' om cuoill maintas vetz los balais
ab qu' el mezeis se balaia.

Dompna que en bon pretz s' enten
deu ben pausar s' entendenssa
en un pro cavallier valen
pois qu' ill conois sa valenssa,
que l' aus amar a presenssa;
que dompna, pois am' a presen,
ja pois li pro ni li valen
no. n dirant mas avinenssa.

Qu' ieu n' ai chausit un pro e gen,
per cui pretz meillur' e gennsa,
larc et adreig e conoissen,
on es sense e conoissenssa.
Prec li que m' aia crezenssa,
ni om no. l puosca far crezen

Comtessa de Dia was probably called Beatriz. According to her vida, she was married to William of Poitiers, but was in love with and sang about Raimbaut d'Aurenga. A fragment of the music that accompanied this is the only surviving transcription of trobairitz song.

1.

I keep my thrive alive by youth and joy,
and youth and joy drive me,
since my boy puts the bliss in bliss
I play and play and live to kiss;
and since I'm real,
he must be too.
I can't see love that strays and wanders—
that's a road my heart can't ponder.

Yes I am so happy, for my man
when he loves the love is oh so fine.
That other boy who helped us meet—
send good things to light his world.
And if you don't think I tell the truth,
you can bind a broom,
and with the broom be swept away.[56]

Any girl who knows what's up
puts her affection in her confection,
in a dude who won't go for mass defection.
And as soon as he proves to fill her cup,
she lets go risk and meets him face to face;
any guy worth any time at all,
speaks true of her who shed grace
to trade and profit in their give and take.

I've picked a posh and entitled guy
whose skill is fruit and makes things ripe.
He gives, doesn't lie, and seems to know why;
he has brains and sees through hype.
If he will just believe in me
and ignore the lies from spies who say

---

[56] Is this a proverb? Maybe. The literal translation is "One often picks the brooms with which one sweeps oneself," or one is usually responsible for one's own undoing.

qu' ieu fassa vas lui faillimen,
sol non trob en lui faillensa.

Amics, la vostra valenssa
sabon li pro e li valen
per qu' ieu de mantenen
si. us plai vostra mantenenssa.

I would dare to make another move
if he left me here not to live but be.

Baby, your value
is seen by all who see,
and so I'm asking please,
stay and take care of me.

2.

A chantar m' er de so qu' ieu non volria,
tant me rancur de luis cui sui amia,
car l' am mais que nuilla ren que sia;
vas lui no. m val merces ni cortesia,
ni ma beltatz ni mos pretz ni mos sens,
c' atressi. m sui enganad' e trahia
com degr' esser, s' ieu fos desavinens.

D' aisso. m. connort car anc non fi faillenssa,
amics, vas vos per nuilla captenenssa,
anz vos am mais non fetz Seguis Valenssa;
e platz me mout quez eu d' amar vos venssa,
lo mieus amics, car etz lo plus valens;
mi faitz orguoill en ditz et en parvenssa,
e si etz francs vas totas autras gens.

Be. m meravill com vostre cors s' orguoilla,
amics, vas me, per qu' ai razon qu' ieu m duoilla;
non es ges dreitz c' autr' amors vos mi tuoilla
per nuilla ren que. us diga ni acuoilla;
e membre vos cals fo. l comenssamens
de nostr' amor! ja Dompnaedieuz non vuoilla
qu' en ma colpa sia. l' departimens.

Proesa grans qu' el vostre cors s' aizina
e lo rics pretz qu' avetz m' en ataina,
c' una non sai, loindana ni vezina,
si vol amar, vas vos no si' aclina;
mas vos, amics, etz ben tant conoissens
que ben devetz conoisser la plis fina;
e membre vos de nostres partimens.

Valer mi deu mos pretz e mos paratges,
e ma beltatz e plus mos fis cortages,
per qu' ieu vos mand lai on es vostr' estatges
esta chansson que me sia messatges;
ieu vuoill saber, lo mieus bel amics gens,
per que vos m' etz tant fers ni tant salvatges;
non said si s' es orguoills o mal talens.

Mas aitan plus vuoill li digas, messatges,
qu' en trop d' orguoill ant gran dan maintas gens.

2.

I sing of things better left unsaid
confessing the rage I feel for him
who I've wanted more than anything.
All my pity and good girl deeds died,
along with my body, soul, and brain
since I've been played the total fool
and used like some old, useless tool.

Here's truth that makes good return:
not even once did I try to burn
him who was Romeo to my Juliet.[57]
So I guess in this I'll win,
since I love better than he can.
Here you are, so cold to me,
and to others, so warm and free.

I knew how I'd live on in sad dread,
the day you grew blind to me.
Why did you let her inside your head,
and give to her what was mine instead?
Remember how we loved at the start!
Don't make me be the one
who breaks us, as you broke my heart.

I know there is real worth in you,
better than money, better than sex.
All the women both far and near
would take their chance to be with you.
But honey, you above all have the sense,
to see that I'm above the rest.
Who makes poems better than we do?

My place should carry some weight,
along with my beauty and my open heart.
I send you, there in your far away state,
this song as messenger and delegate.
I need to know, you cruelly fine friend,
why I deserve such a brutal fate.
It is either pride or spite I offend.

But above all, let these words be the sound
of excess pride knocking you down.

---

[57] *Seguis and Valenssa* was a popular romance whose story is lost.

3.

Estat ai en greu cossirier
per un cavallier qu' ai agut
e vuoil sia totz temps saubut
cum ieu l' ai amat a sobrier;
ara vei qu' ieu sui trahida
car ieu non li donei m' amor
don ai estat en gran error
en lieig e quand sui vestida.

Ben volria mon cavallier
tener un ser en mos bratz nut.
Qu' el s' en tengra per ereubut
sol qu' a lui fezes cosseillier
car plus m' en sui abellida
no fetz Floris de Blanchafor:
ieu l' autrei mon cor e m' amor,
mon sen, mos huoills e ma vida.

Bels amics avinens e bos,
cora. us tenrai en mon poder?
e que jagues ab vos un ser
e qu' ie. us des un bais amoros;
sapchatz, gran talan n' auria
qu' ie. us tengues en luoc del marit,
ab so que m' aguessetz plevit
de far tot so qu' ieu volria.

3.

I've been thrown into hell
because of a man I once called mine,
and this is true now and for all time
since I love him beyond my skill to tell.
So it turns out it was a test,
his quest for sex night and day;
and now I can't stop thinking
yes, all I had to say was *yes*.

Oh, just once had I stroked him,
he'd never ever rise for anyone else;
I'd pull him close and closer and he'd rest,
leaning his head against my breast.
It's true I was happier with him
than any romance you'll recall;[58]
I'll bet this heart for him, I'll bet it all,
my mind, my eyes, my life.

Beautiful boy, so totally cool and kind,
when will you bow to my power?
If I could lie beside you for just one hour,
you'd never be free from our body.
There's nothing I wouldn't give
to have you in my husband's place,
but only if you swear you will always act
with me in mind, no matter what the case.

---

[58] *Floris and Blanchafor* was also a popular romance of the period.

4.

Fin ioi me don' alegranssa,
per qu' eu chan plus gaiamen,
e no m' o teing a pensanssa,
ni a negun pennsamen,
car sai que son a mon dan
fals lausengier e truan,
e lor mals diz non m' esglais:
anz en son dos tanza plus gaia.

En mi non an ges fianssa
li lauzengier mal dizen,
c' om non pot aver honranssa
qu' a ab els acordamen;
qu' ist son d' altrestal semblan
com la niuols que s' espan
qu. l solels en pert sa raia,
per qu' eu non am gent savaia.

E vos, gelos mal parlan,
no. s cuges que m' an tarzan,
que iois e iovenz no. m plaia,
per tal que dols vos deschaia.

4.

True love carries its share of joy,
so these words sing too of joy,
and I don't worry or fret,
or give it the time of day,
though gossips hurt us.
Their trash talk doesn't scare me;
I laugh and laugh at the crap they say.

Those foul-mouthed love killers
earn zero trust from us.
And you who want an open life
won't believe their lies in honesty.
They are clouds that spread,
spread, and spread across a sky,
until the sun is blotted out.
They don't deserve to be talked about.

And you, my whining spouse,
I've seen the way to leave.
I lean towards joy and new life,
away from grief that named me wife.

ANONYMOUS

BALADA

A l' entrade del tens clar—*eya*
pir ioie recomençar—*eya*
e pir ialous irritar—*eya*
vol la regine mostra
k' ele est si amourouse.
A la vi, a la vie, ialous!
Lassaz nos, lassaz nos
ballar entre nos, entre nos.

Ele a fait pir tot mandar—*eya*
non sie iusq' a la mar—*eya*
pucele ni bachelar—*eya*
que tuit non venguent dançar
en la dance ioiouse.
A la vi, a la vie, ialous!
Lassaz nos, lassaz nos
ballar entre nos, entre nos.

Lo reis I vent d' autre part—*eya*
pir la dance destorbar—*eya*
que il est en cremetar—*eya*
que on ne li vuelle emblar
la regine avrillouse.
A la vi, a la vie, ialous!
Lassaz nos, lassaz nos
ballar entre nos, entre nos.

Mas pir neient lo vol far—*eya*
k' ele n' a soing de viellart—*eya*
mais d' un legeir bachelar—*eya*
ki ben sache solaçar
la donne savorouse.
A la vi, a la vie, ialous!
Lassaz nos, lassaz nos
ballar entre nos.

This balada *is a song that may been sung by people at out-door spring celebrations. It may have been used to worship Flora and Venus.*

At the start of Spring—*la la*
to begin again in joy—*la la*
her envy left to things or Kings—*la la*
Regina begins to show
the Tao of her desire.
To life, to this paradise
Leave us, leave us,
Dancing together, together.

She's called everyone—*la la*
from the land to the sea—*la la*
all new girls and boys—*la la*
to come to her for free
and dance the happy dance.
To life, to this paradise
Leave us, leave us
Dancing together, together.

Roy comes from another where—*la la*
to destroy what he'll never share—*la la*
the April Queen Regine—*la la*
the dance, the sex
stolen freely from the air.
To life, to this paradise
Leave us, leave us
Dancing, dancing together.

King Roy can't wreck her or the dance—*la la*
Regina only breaks—*la la*
for love, for real trance—*la la*
for the perfect boy whose touch
is god's mist, sun's hair, divinity's thrust.
To life, to this paradise
Leave us, leave us
Dancing, dancing together.

Qui donc la veist dançar—*eya*
e son gent cors deportar—*eya*
ben puist dire de vertat—*eya*
k' el mont non aie sa par
la regine ioiouse.
A la vi', a la vie, ialous!
Lassaz nos lassaz nos
ballar entre nos, entre nos.

See how she is dancing then—*la la*
all mist all sun all god began—*la la*
we who share her now have been—*la la*
inside a day made whole again
inside Regina's new found body.
To life, to this paradise
Leave us, leave us,
Dancing together, together.

ALAMANDA AND GIRAUT DE BORNELH

TENSO

S' ie. us quier conseill, bell' ami' Alamanda,
no. l me vedetz, qu' om cochatz lo. us demanda,
que so m' a dich vostra dompna truanda
que loing sui fors issitz de sa comanda,
que so que. m det m' estrai er e.m desmanda;
que. m cosseillatz?
qu' a pauc lo cors totz d' ira no. m abranda,
tan fort en sui iratz.

Per Dieu, Giruat, jes aissi tot a randa
volers d' amics noi.s fai ni nois.s garanda,
que, si l' uns faill, l' autre coven que blanda,
que lor destrics noi.s cresca ni s' espanda;
e s' ela. us ditz d' aut puoig que sia landa,
vos la 'n crezatz,
e plassa vos lo bes e. l mals qu' il manda,
qu' aissi seretz amatz.

Non puos mudar que contr' orguoill non gronda
ja siatz vos donzella bell' e blonda;
pauc d' ira. us notz e paucs jois vos aonda,
mas jes non etz primieira ni segonda.
Ieu que. m tem fort d' est ira que. m confonda—
vos me lauzatz,
si. m sent perir, que. m tenga plus vas l' onda:
mal cre que. m capdellatz.

Si m' enqueretz d' aital razon prionda,
per Dieu, Giraut, non sai, com vos responda;
vos m' apellatz de leu cor jauzionda—
mais vuoill pelar mon prat qu' autre. l mi tonda;

Alamanda was probably Alamanda de Castelnou, who was born around 1160. In all likelihood, she spent her childhood, prior to her marriage to Guilhelm de Castelnou, at the court of Count Raimon V of Toulouse where she would have made this tenso *with Guiraut de Bornelh. Bornelh (1138-1215) was a troubadour at the court of the Viscount of Limoges. He is credited as the inventor of* trobar leu, *or the "light" style of troubadour poetry.*

This is need to know, pretty little A.,
don't make me suss, since I'm reject-man.
Since your lying friend's let loose her grasp
what she gave, she took back, just like that.
What can I say?
I'm so pissed,
I can feel my body
bursting into flames.

God damn, G., what you want—she doesn't care.
This is a game of give and take, so what you lose
just give it up, and keep the show going,
or your bad now will keep on growing.
If she says that high is low
believe her
and buy the good and bad she throws—
no other way to get her love, that's sure.

I can't stop coming up against her pride
when I see you here so blonde, so cake.
The pain slays, and bliss sinks my ache,
and I'm still not at first or second base.
I'm worrying this rage will kill me:
you're sweet and say I'm rad
but I know—I'm closer to the waves,[59]
no matter how your play makes my day.

When you come to me with whys so deep,
Jeez-God, G, I don't know how to speak.
You say I have such a happy heart—
I just want to mow my field before X reaps there![60]

---

[59] A suicide wish? *Onda* is wave in the original.

[60] The trobairitz seems to be wishing for some condition of autonomy here before she is inevitably married off; or perhaps she is feeling desire for the troubadour and so failing in her role as friendly intermediary.

que s' ie. us era del plaich far desironda,
vos escercatz;
com son bels cors vos esdui' e.us resconda,
ben par com n' etz cochatz.

Donzell', oimais non siatz tant parlieira,
qu' il m' a mentit mais de cinc vetz primieira;
cujatz vos doncs qu' ieu totz temps lo sofieira?
Semblaria qu' o fezes per nescieira.
D' autr; aimstat ai talan qu' ie. us enquieira,
si no. us calatz;
meillor cosseil dava na Berengieira
que vos non m' en donatz.

Lora vei ieu, Giraut, qu' ela. us o mieira,
car l' apelletz camjairitz ni leugueira;
pero cujatz que del plaich vos enquieira?
Ieu non cuig jes qu' il sia tant mainieira:
ans er oimais sa proeza derreia,
que que. us digatz,
si. s destrenh tant que contra vos sofieira
trega ni fi ni patz.

Bella, per Dieu, non perga vostr' ajuda;
ja sabetz vos com mi fo covenguda;
s' ieu ai faillit per l' ira qu' ai agida,
no.m tenga dan; s' anc sentitz com leu muda
cors d' amador, bella, e s' anc sentitz fotz druda,
del plaich penstatz!
Qu' ieu sui be mortz, s' enaissi l' ai perduda;
mas no. lh o descobratz!

Seign' en Giraut, ja n' agr' ieu fin volguda,
mas ella ditz qu 'a dreich s' es irascuda,
qu' autra n prejetz com fols tot a saubuda
que non la val ni vestida ni nuda;
noi fara doncs, si no. us gic, que vencuda,
s' autra 'n prejatz?
Be. us en valrai et ai la. us manteguda,
si mais no. us I mesclatz.

If I wanted to help you make peace with her
I'd say find out why she's mad at you,
since she's hiding herself from view,
and your pain is clear, that's for sure.

Little miss, now you are talking shit.
She lied to me first and then five times more.
I'm not down with playing the fool;
if you don't chill and keep this cool,
I'll make you find me another sweet trace.
I got more up front advice from N.B.[61]
than any words you give about love's case.
You think I can take this and not keep score?

So you say she's playing you the fool,
and now you'll look for some other rule;
why would she want to get back with you?
I don't think you've broken her yet;
from now on the laws are all on hold,
no matter what you say to look bold.
She is so mad at you that she won't hear
your silence or pleas, or any peace treaty.

Honey, for Christ's sake, don't leave me now—
you're the one who gets what's up with me.
If I've been wrong in getting so mad,
just call it my bad; if you've ever felt how fast
love can change, or if you've wanted it to last,
honey, please just find some way.
I'm a dead man if I lose her now;
please don't let her hear what I just said.

Mr. G., you know I don't want your love to end,
but she says she's the one who should be mad,
since you're toying in front of all our friends,
with one who is nothing next to her, dressed or nude;
she'd look weak if she didn't dump you,
while you're loving another and aren't true.
But I'll tell her you're cool as I always have,
if you swear to not act like that.

---

[61] Lady Berengieira was probably another noble woman.

Bella, per Dieu, si de lai n' etz crezuda,
per me l' o affiatz!

Ben o farai, mas, quan vos er renduda
s' amors, non la. us toillatz.

Beautiful, for God's sake, if she trusts you,
promise her I'll again be true.

Ok, but when she gives her love once more,
you'll be through if you again let it go.

AZALAIS DE PORCAIRAGES

CANSO

Ar em al freg temps vengut
quel gels el neus e la faingna
e. l aucellet estan mut,
c' us de chantar non s' afraingna;
e son see li ram pels plais—
que flors ni foilla noi nais,
ni rossignols noi crida,
que l' am e mai me reissida.

Tant ai lo cors deseubut,
per qu' ieu soi a totz estraingna,
e sai que l' om a perdut
que vos non m' en donatz.
molt plus tost que non gasaingna;
e s' ieu faill ab motz verais,
d' Aurenga me moc l' esglais,
per qu' ieu m' estauc esbaida
e 'n pert solatz en partida.

Dompna met mot mal s' amor
que ab ric ome plaideia,
ab plus aut de vavassor;
e s' il o fai, il folleia,
car so diz om en Veillai
que ges per ricor non vai,
e dompna que n' es chauzida
en tenc per envilanida.

Amic ai de gran valor
que sobre toz seignoreia,
e non a cor trichador
vas me, que m' amor m' autreia.
Ieu dic que m' amors l' eschai,
e cel que dis que non fai,
Dieus li don mal' escarida,
qu ieu m' en teing fort per guerida.

Azalais was born in the 1140s at the castle of Portiragnes and was a neighbor of Gui Guerrejat, the recipient of her song, who lived northeast of Beziers. Her vida describes her as a well-educated noblewoman from the region of Montpellier. She had poetic ties to the court of Raimbaut d'Aurenga, who is the lost, possibly dead lover named in the poem, who presided over one of the most important centers of poetry in Occitania.

Now we come to our winter phase[62]
when the mud, the ice and snow,
and cock song dies of age
(not one wakes up to crow):
the bush and branch are dry cups.
Leaves and blooms all fall down,
the nightingale makes no sound
nor May song that once did wake him up.

My heart makes such a riot,
I hurt everyone the same.
Loss is an easier act
than gain; since I'm the one they blame
let's go with facts:
my pain comes from a fine man's name.
And so I'm wide open, I'm bust,
zero life left in our lust.

Love wages a losing deal
in a girl's war with rich tools,
with any dudes, except her slaves:
Little Every-girl is a fool.
The people around my city
think love and money don't mix,
and the girl that money kitties
loses credit in that fix.

I have a huge and famous friend,
a giant cloud over other men,
the sweet he sends me can't just end;
his love won't name me victim.
So I give, and give it back,
and whosoever says I don't or can't,
God sink their luck in His rant—
I'll make my way and take no chance.

---

[62] The springtime opening, which was prominent in poems of male troubadours, only appears here and in the anonymous "Quan Vei Los Praz Verdesir" in the trobaritz's corpus.

Bels amics, de bon talan
son ab vos toz jornz en gatge,
cortez' e de bel semblan,
sol no. m demandes outratge;
tost en venrem a l' assai,
qu' en vostra merce. M metrai:
vos m' avetz la fe plevida,
que no. m demandes faillada.

A Dieu coman Bel Esgar
e plus la ciutat d' Aurenza,
e Gloriet' e. Caslar,
e lo seignor de Proenza
e tot can vol mon ben lai,
e l' arc on son fag l' assai.
Celui perdiei c' a ma vida,
e' n serai toz jorns marrida.

Joglar, que avetz cor gai,
ves Narbona portatz lai
ma chanson ab la fenida
lei vui joi e jovens guida.

Dear friend, I'll wait and stay.
A girl is made by feel—
your look, your words make my way.
We'll see how much we pay.
My life is in your hands:
you said you would keep us right
as long as we keep it real,
so please do, and let's not fight.

I hand over the bank to God
and the city of blank,
all those prophets of buy and trade,
the CEOs of all my days,
all of you who my value made,
by outing me in the writing on the wall.
I've lost Mr. Big who owned my life;
nothing else will be forgiven.

Singer, who believes in joy,
bring my song into the city,
a song made for her pity,
whose guides too were joy.

CLARA D'ANDUZA

TENSO

En greu esmai et en greu pessamen
an mes mon cor et an granda error
li lauzengier e. l fals devinador,
abaissadorde joi e de joven;
quar vos qu' ieu am mais que res qu' el mon sia
an fait de me departir e lonhar,
si qu' ieu no. us puesc vezer ni remirar,
don muer de dol, d' ira e de feunia.

Ve que. m blasma vostr' amor ni. m defen
non pot en far e re mon cor meillor,
ni. l dous deair qu' ieu ai de vos major
ni l' enveja ni. l dezir ni. l talen;
e non es om, tan mos enemics sia,
si. l n' aug dir ben, que non lo tenh' en car,
e, si 'n ditz mal, mais no. m pot dir ni far
neguna re que a plazer me sia.

Ja no. us donetz, bel amics, espaven
que ja ves vos aja cor trichador,
ni qu' ie. Us camge per nul autr' amador;
qu' amors que. m te per vos en sa bailia
vol que mon cor vos estui e vos gar,
e farai o; e s' ieu pogues emblar
mon cor, tals l' a que jamais non l' auria.

Amics, tan ai d' ira e de feunia
quar no os vey, que quan ieu cug chantar,
planh e sospir, per qu' ieu non puesc so far
ab mas coblas que. l cors complir volria.

Clara d'Anduza lived in the first part of the 13th century, and is thought to have been a nobelwoman in the house of Anduza, a court that supported troubadours. Her work is linked with Lanfrancs Cigala and Azalais d'Altier, among others.

The dull weight I carry inside
was buried there by killers of joy,
by voyeurs and gossips and lying spies;
my heart a thick thing now, without my boy.
For you were the one I loved the best,
and as their slurs pushed you from my side,
the time now comes to welcome death,
rather than live in awful resentment.

If any will speak well of you again,
she is sister I once called foe;
just so she who says a word against you,
will then never again be called my friend.
And all the small patrons of your fault,
who blame or ban my certain love for you,
they are powerless to instruct my heart
as no other need has proven me true.

And if you should doubt me, handsome friend,
and think my song plays to another man,
I'd never trade you, don't think that I can,
though hundreds may try to buy my hand.
This feeling for you has cast its spell.
It took hold one day in my core,
and taught me to lock and guard you well,
since your claim on me can't be ignored.

Without you I am so bitter, so mad,
my tears drown out the song that I might sing.
I'm deaf—there's no music in anything,
not even these words, where love once lived.

JOHAN DE PENNAS AND ANONYMOUS DOMNA

TENSO

Un guerrier per alegrar
vuelh comensar car m' agensa,
que non lo dey plus celar,
trop l' auray tengut en pensa;
e guereiaray d' amor,
en domens de ma guerieira
a trobat guereiador
que guereia volontieira.

Guerier, ben vuelh guereiar
ab vos d' amor ses failhensa,
car—sapchas—non puesc trobar
hom de milhor entendensa
ni sia plus fin aimador
ni mielh sapcha la karieira
de ben amar per amor
ni tengua sa laus entieira.

Guerieira, sobrelauzer
mi voles per benvolensa;
ben vos vuelh dir ses duptar
—e iur vos per ma crezensa—
que vos es de beutat flor,
que non say, hon ieu mi quieira,
en tharascon bellazor
que miels del dart d' amor fieira.

Mon gueier, cortes d' amar,
sapchas que gran penedensa
sufri car no' us aus mostrar
l' amistat gran de valensa
qu' ieu vos port, car gra secor
mi for a si la manieira
no fos del lauzengador
maldizen qu' es trop sobrieira.

Johan de Pennas was active in the 13th century.

Because I'm happy, I'll sing a song,
because I'm happy or anyway glad,
and so don't hide what drives me mad,
the dear thoughts I held too long.
I will let go and sing of love,
the day after my friend, after my foe
calls for war in open field;
and shows me his friend, me his foe;
how two can bend so love won't go.

Soldier, yes this is my war to wage
in word, in thought, for its love I gauge;
and though it's true I may never find
a man who sees with such full mind,
who follows along an open range,
and I from myself am at last estranged,[63]
when I turn up glad to fight or yield.

Woman warrior, your applause and praise
offer too much to me because you are kind;
the you I see now in my mind
—the lover through time which makes my case—
shapes flower petals through boundless space.
And I will never see, wherever I turn,
another form more perfect in any place
whose blossom burns light inside a trace.

My rebel slave, enabler for love,
so many days I have lived with this pain
because I could never tell you
what I wanted was love, not just in name,
but something clean and basic, much like dew.
The talkers around, tellers of custom,
they couldn't understand this dread feeling,
to fear love that would leave me kneeling.

---

[63] The Cathar Perfect had to reach self-detachment in order to achieve salvation. Here the anonymous *Domna* equates the pinnacle of *fin'amor* with likewise such detachment, a theme in the most realized poems of the troubadours' oeuvre. The poem continues in further mystical terms, where the basic elements of nature—light, dew—are understood in terms of their feelings. "She" has achieved *consolamentum*, which he recognizes, and is thus also free.

Ma guerieira, am pres clar,
plena de gran conoissensa,
no vulhas per so laisar
qu' ieu suy en vostra plevensa;
car qui am' a sa honor
leialmens ni vertadieira
non deu pas aver temor
de perona lauzengieira.

Seray lial guerrierira,
car vos portas per lauzor
de savia Guerier, per vostra valor
vos la bannieira.

My warrior woman, I love one you,
you are sage without end, old wisdom.
Your knowledge builds its own freedom,
for what I found in you now grows in me too.
My honor writes of new trust in me,
close to what I am in fact, close in truth—
the fear that filled my hours and days now free,
from rumor's choke chain, scandal's decree.

My warrior, the song is wager of your worth.
And I will be true inside its determined rhyme,
for the sense you sang now is mine.
My flag, your token and your prize.

LOMBARDA AND BERNAUT ARNAUT

TENSO

1.

Lombards volgr' eu esser per na Lombarda,
qu' Alamanda no. m plaz tan ni Giscarda,
qar ab sos oiltz plaisenz tan jen mi garda
qe par qe. m don s' amor, mas trop me tarda.

> Quar bel vezer
> e mon plaiser
> ten e bel ris en garda,
> c' om no. ls ne pod mover.

Seigner Jordan, se vos lais Alamagna
Frans' e Piteus, Normandi' e Bretagna,
be me devez laisar senes mesclagna
e Lombardi' e Livorn' e Lomagna

> E si. M valez
> eu per un dez
> valdre. us ab leis qu' estragna
> es de tot avol prez.

> Mirail de prez,
> c' onor avez,
> ges per vila no. s fragna
> l' amors en qe.m tenez.

Lombarda is identified as a 13th-century Gascon in the vida of Bernaut Arnaut. Bernaut was a troubadour in the court of Armagnac.

1.

I'd like to be the L-Bard for L-Barda girl,
I get her more than A. Manda or G. Carda girls;[64]
I kow-tow when she eyes me,
but cube it since her sweet is not for free.

> For her beauty and her good time,
> is all inside my good time,
> and all three she's locked and keyed
> inside a laurel tree.

Mr. J., if I comp you G. town,
F., P., N. and B., town,
when all's said and done, you see me
all 3 L. towns, my new trinity.

> And if you want rich,
> I'll see your rich,
> and raise you some for Her
> whose taste will make me pure.

> Lady Luck, you're a mirror
> where we see things clearly.
> Don't let that Mr. All Talk
> steal the sweet that brought us nearly...

---

[64] A reference to Alamanda. Arnaut is wagering with "Lord Jordan," whom he sees as a rival for Lombarda's love.

2.

No. m volgr' aver per Bernard na Bernarda
e per n' Arnaut n' Arnauda appellada,
e grans merces, seigner, car vos agrada
c' ab tala doas domnas m' aves nommada.

    Voil qem digaz
    cals mais vos plaz
    ses cuberta
    e.l mirail on miratz.

Car lo mirailz e no veser descorda
tan mon acord c' ab pauc no. l desacorda,
mas can record so qu' l meus noms recorda,
en bon acord totz mons pensars s' acorda.

    Mas del cor pes
    on l' aves mes,
    que sa maiso ni borda
    no vei, que las taises.

2.

I'm glad I wasn't called Bernada for Bernaut
and that I wasn't made Arnauda for you Arnaut;
so thanks but no thanks B., since it gives you joy
to name me side by side with two such girls.

      I want to know
      the truth inside of you,
      which of three you want and who
      stares from the mirror where you choose.

The mirror mirage so stunts
my rhyme it nearly stops it,
but then I remember my name is proof,
and body and mind call a truce.

      But your home place,
      where your heart lies?
      Your house, your fireside, is hid,
      and I can't hear what they say.[65]

---

[65] Lombarda was the only trobairitz to write in *trobar clus*, the so-called hermetic or "closed" style of the troubadours. It seems pretty clear she's making fun of Arnaut, suggesting that since he's named two other women in the poem beside her, his song has no merit.

TIBORS DE SARENOM

CANSO (FRAGMENT)

Bels dous amics, ben von posc en ver dir
que anc non fo qu' ieu estes ses desir
pos vos conven que. us tenc per fin aman;
ni anc no fo qu' leu non agues talan,
bels dous amics, qui' ieu soven no us vezes;
ni anc no fo sazons que m' en pentis,
ni anc no se vos n' anes iratz,
qu' ieu agues joi tro que fostez tornatz;
ni...

Tibors may have been the sister of Raimbaut d'Aurenga, though her vida implies that she lived in the 13th century. This is the oldest work in the trobairitz corpus.

I can't lie to you, love—
I am so far gone,
since you took me where no one else can;
nor will a time come you won't be my man
and I will stop craving you each day;
nor, your wish list I won't pay,
nor, when I let you go away mad
did I ever feel joy 'til you came back;
Nor...

ISABELLA AND ELIAS CAIREL

TENSO

N' Elias Cairel, de l' amor
qu' ieu e vos soliam aver
voil, si. us platz, que. m digatz lo ver,
per que l' avetz cambiad' aillor;
que vostre chanz non vai si com solia,
et anc vas vos no. m sui salvatz un dia,
ni vos d' amor no. m demandetz anc tan
qu' ieu non fezes tot al vostre coman.

Ma domn' Isabella, valor
joi e pretz e sen e saber
soliatz quec jorn mantener,
e s' ieu en dizia lauzor
en mon chantar, no. l dis per drudaria,
mas per honor e pro qu' ieu n' atendia,
si com joglars fai de domna prezan;
mas chascun jorn m' etz anada cambian.

N' Elias Cairel, amador
non vi mais de vostre voler,
qui cambies domna per aver,
e s' ieu en disses desonor
ieu n' ai dig tant de be qu' om no. l creiria;
mas ben podetz doblar vosta follia:
de mi vos dic qu' ades vau mailluran,
mas endreig vos non ai cor ni talan.

Domna, ieu faria gran follor,
e' estes gair' en vostre poder,
e ges per tal no. m desesper,
s' anc tot non aic pro ni honor;
vos remanretz tals com la genz vos cria,
et ieu irei vezer ma bell' amia
e. l sieu gen cors grail' e ben estan,
que no. m a cor menzongier ni truan.

Isabella is either Isabella de Montferrat or Isabella de Malaspina. She lived in the early years of the 13th century. Elias Cairel served the crusader Boniface I of Montferrat in Greece. A goldsmith by trade and a joglar who travelled the world for many years, Pound translates his vida as follows: "Elias Cairel was of Sarlat; ill he sang, ill he composed, ill he played the fiddle and worse he spoke..."

Where's it gone Elias C., our love—
come clean and say where it's run—
say, please, why we've undone
the groove that grew between us.
Your songs don't croon the way they did,
though I came to you and wasn't stingy;
I gave you love on demand,
since your word was my whole gig.

O, what the hell Isabel.
You were cool then,
happy, strong, a wise, funny friend;
but when I sang what you did well,
you'd be dumb if you couldn't tell,
what I sang, I sang for money.
Actors, they learn how to act,
but you, you always change and that's a fact.

Elias C., this is a first,
since it's you, not me, who's dumb.
All that swag you trade for love
is junk; the best in your song,
singing of me, is live in memory.
Go ahead, double down your crazy!
Without you, life's amazing.
We're through. I've no more use for you.

Lady, I'd be crazy to remain
one more day in your domain;
but I really don't care
if I don't have rep or money.
You're just a statue built by men,
so I'm off to see my pretty friend
whose fine skin doesn't smell funny,
whose heart can't be bought or lent.

N' Elias Cairel fegnedor
resemblatz segon mon parer,
com hom qu.s feing de dol aver
de so dont el non sent dolor.
Si. m creziatz, bon conseil vos daria:
que tornassetz estar en la badia,
e no. us auzei anc mais dir mon semblan,
mas pregar n' ei lo patriarch' Ivan.

Domn' Isabel, en refreitor
non estei anc mattin ni ser,
mas vos n' auretz aimais lezer,
qu' en breu temps perdretz la color;
estier mon grat mi faitz dir vilania,
et ai mentit, qu' ieu non crei qu' el mond sia
domna tant pros ni ab beutat tant gran
com vos avetz, per qu' ieu ai agut dan.

Si. us plazia, n' Elias, ieu volria
que. m disessetz, quals es la vostr' amia,
e digatz lo, m e no I anetz doptan,
qu' ieu. Us en valrai, s' ela val ni a sen tan.

Domna, vos m' enqueretz de gran follia,
que per razon s' amistat en perdria,
e per paor que lauzengier mi fan,
pero non aus descubrir.

Elias C., you are the biggest dick
I've ever laid eyes upon;
like a man who says he's sick
and whose pain is just a con.
Listen to what I say, if you can:
go away and hide—
don't say my name again
but to pray to Saints who know why.

Isabella, I'll never sit down to eat
in a monk's retreat
though you will often,
now your looks have begun to soften.
It's because of you I'm a dick,
and tell you these lies, because you girl[66]
are the best in the world;
your beauty has made me sick.

Elias, tell me if you will
which new lady is your thrill:
just tell me, don't be scared,
so I can judge her and be fair.

Izzie, I can't risk such a thing,
then she'll leave me suffering;
the twisted sisters will start to chatter
and what *I* want? It won't matter.

---

[66] Elias apparently feels he's been defeated in the terms of *trobar*, and so essentially turns his criticism of Isabella to praise. This is a characteristic move in many troubadour poems.

MARIA DE VENTADORN AND GUI D'USSEL

TENSO

Gui d' Ussel, be. m pesa de vos,
car vos etz laissatz de chantar,
e car vos i volgra tornar,
per que sabetz d' aitals razos,
vuoill que. m digatz, si dei far egalmen
dompna per drut, can lo quier francamen,
cum el per lieis tot cant taing ad amor
segon los dreitz que tenon l' amador.

Dompna na Maria, tenssos
e tot chant cuiava laissar,
mas aoras non puosc estar
qu' ieu non chant als vostres somos;
e respon vos de la dompna breumen
que per son drut deu far comunalmen
cum el per pieis, ses garda de ricor:
qu' en dos amics non deu aver maior.

Gui, tot so don es cobeitos
deu drutz ab merce demandar,
e dompna deu l' o autreiar,
mas ben deu esgardar sazos;
e. l drutz deu far precs e comandamen
cum per amig' e per dompn' eissamen,
e dompna deu a son drut far honor
cum ad amic, mas non cum a seignor.

Dompna, sai dizon de mest nos
que, pois zue dompna vol amar,
egalmen deu son drut onrar,
pois egalmen son amoros;
e s' esdeven que l' am plus finamen,
e. l faich e. l dich en deu far aparen,
e si ell' a fals cor ni trichador,
ab vel semblan deu cobir sa follor.

Maria de Ventadorn was the daughter of Lord Raimon II of Torna. The second wife of Viscount Eble V of Ventadorn, she is the lady most praised in the poems of the troubadours. She entered the cloister of Grandmont in 1221 with her husband. Gui D'Ussel was an early-13ᵗʰ-century troubadour from Limousin.

G., you said good-bye to all that sings,
said *adieu* to songs and things,
you who of all know most what is true—
leaving us the new rules to decode.
A question now to make it clear:
does a girl state it man to man,
or a man bow down to a girl,
and where's a book that maps that world?

Maria, I gave the map to you,
and now in the ash of my *adieu*,
here you are back to tune
the old songs we crooned?
No one's ever been on top,
woman, man, girl and boy;
we are fire in our own laps
when we lose romance's script.

Guy, lovers speak for their desire
to say it straight; there's no joy otherwise.
And girls say yes to his requests
when ecstasy is her recompense.
For the sake of her, he's free to give,
because she is both his friend and star,
even though she see him the same as friend,
not the light that leads her from afar.

Maria, every book I read says
desire makes men and women equal,
so when a girl wants to name the day,
she should be the one to make the call.
If she finds she loves him more,
let her words show who she adores;
but if she cheats and sleeps with others,
just smile and keep it undercover.

Gui d' Uissel, ges d' aitals razos
non son li drut al comenssar,
anz ditz chascus, can vol preiar,
"Dompna, voillatz que. us serva francamen
cum lo vostr' om," et ell' enaissi. l pren;
Eu vo jutge per dreich a trahitor,
si. s. rend pariers ei. s det per servidor.

Dompna, so es plaich vergoignos,
ad ops de dompna razonr,
que cellui non teigna per par
a cui a faich un cor de dos.
O vos diretz, e no. us estara gen,
que. l drutz la deu amar plus finamen,
o vos diretz q' il son par entre lor,
pois ren no. il deu drutz mas qant per amor.

But G., it's never that way at the start,
when their fling is new and it's so hot
—though they both pretend that they are not—
when he promises things later forgot:
"Girl you can have me all now for free,"
and so she loved him then without a fee.
He can't be both her man and her slave.
I don't see the logic in what you say.

Maria, talking with you, I see red.
You fight to be the one on the top,
who says when to start and when to stop,
to one who came freely to your bed.
It's time to admit what you've said:
that either a man can love you only as friend,
or be the one who most wants to score.
And so the new rules rewrite the old.

ANONYMOUS

Dieus sal la terra e' l pais
on vostre cors es ni estai,
on q' eu sia mos cors es lai
qe sai no n' es om poderos;
aissi volgr' eu qe' l cors laid fos,
qi qe sai s' en fezes parliers,
mais n' am un joi que fos entiers
qi qe s' en fai tan enveios.

Nothing is known about the author of this poem.

God wrote the earth and space
where you can be found;[67]
Wherever I am, my heart is in that place,
for here I can't be bound;
So I wish my body was closer,
in spite of chatter here;
I prefer my joy from there
to one who keeps my body near.

---

[67] *Vostre cors* may be your heart, body or self. The poet is at pains to distinguish between heart and body. Her heart is with her lover, while her body is with her husband (*poderos, envois*).

ANONYMOUS

SIRVENTES

No puesc mudar no digua mon vejaire
d' aisso dont ai al cor molt gran error
et er me molt mal e greu a retraire,
quar aquist antic trobador
que 'n son passat, dic que son fort peccaire,
qu' ilh an mes lo segl' en error
que an dig mal de domnas a prezen
e trastug cilh qu' o auzon crezo' ls en
et autreyon tug que ben es semblansa,
et aissi an mes los seg' l en erransa.

E tug auist que eron bon trobaire,
tug se fenhon per leal amador,
mas ieu sai be que non es fis amaire
nuls hom que digual mal d' amor;
enans vos dic qu' es ves amor bauzaire
e fai l' uzatge al traitor
aicel que de so, on plus fort s' aten,
plus en ditz mal aissi tot a prezen,
quar negus hom, s' avia tota Fransa,
no pot ses don' aver gran benestansa.

E jal nuls home que sia bon aire
no sufrira quom en digua folhor,
mas silh que son vas amor tric e vaire
ho auzon e s' en tenon ab lor;
qu' En Marcabrus, a ley de predicaire
quant es en glezia ho orador
que di gran mal de la gen mescrezen,
et el ditz mal de donas eyssamen;
e dic vos be que non l' es gran honransa
ce qui ditz mal d' aisso don nays enfansa.

Ia no sia negus meraveillaire
s' ieu aisso dic ni vuelh mostrar alhor
que quascus home deu razonar son fraire
e queia domna sa seror,

The unknown author of this sirventes *may have been a trobairitz in the court of Maria de Ventadorn.*

(in memory of Sylvia Plath)

The poets who wrote our Book
are dead and our fiction is their fault.
They were those who taught
that women are slave and master,
to audiences predisposed to hear.
Our status early met disaster,
and what was posed haunts us to this year.
And because I have more than one mouth to tell,
I tell it well, and as our sister said:
"I do it so it feels like hell."

The fable goes that good poets
are always the best lovers,
but some old poems serve to show it—
love breeds misogyny under covers.
A girl is not a nation
but the worst would have it so;
the canon a spy's oblation
and poets' lies culture's code.
See how the more he strives for love,
things for Our girl are worse to go.

If you think that girls cause love to go wrong
hear the warning in my anti love song;
a group of men is indeed a club—
perhaps it's time
they open their meeting.
M.'s poems play like opinion polls,
where different faiths and women alike
take the blame for what is worst
on earth, assigning the greatest crime
to our mothers, simply for our births.

I'll say what's been said before
by the truth that hides in history,
that each should defend her sisters
and her brothers—it's no mystery,

quar Adams fo lo nostre premier paire
e avem Damnidieu ad auctor;
e s' ieu per so velh far razonamen
a las domnas, no m' o reptes nien,
quar dona deu az autra far onransa
e per aisso ai 'n ieu dig ma semblansa.

since together we are woman and man
and in each other have made the race.
But this is my poem,
where girls come first;
standing together we make our case,
and as for me, I could have done worse.[68]

---

[68] The poem critiques the misogyny in troubadour poems, specifically that of the moralist Marcabru (1130-1149), as well as the poets' public who could be tricked into believing things that were false.

SELECTED BIBLIOGRAPHY

Aurell i Cardon, Martín. "La détérioration du statut de la femme aristocratique en Provence (Xe-XIIIe siècles)." *Le Moyen Age* 91 (1985): 6-32
_____. *Une famille de la noblesse provençale au moyen âge: Les Porcelet*, Avignon: Aubanel, 1986.

Bénétrix, Paul. *Les femmes troubadours: Notes d'histoire littéraire*. Agen: Lenthéric, 1889.

Bogin, Meg. *The Women Troubadours*. New York and London: W.W. Norton and Co., 1980.

Bruckner, Matilda T., Laurie Shepard and Sarah White, eds. *Songs of the Women Troubadours*. New York and London: Garland, 1995.

Derrida, Jacques. "What is Relevant Translation?" Trans. Lawrence Venutti. *Critical Inquiry* 27: 174-200, 2001.

Dronke, Peter. "The Provençal *Trobairitz*: Castelloza." In *Medieval Women Writers*. Ed. Katharina M. Wilson. Athens: University of Georgia Press, 1984.
_____. *Women Writers of the Middle Ages: A Critical Study of Texts from Perpetua (+203) to Marguerite Porete (+1310)*. Cambridge: Cambridge University Press, 1984.

Graham-Leigh, Elaine. *The Southern French Nobility and the Albigensian Crusade*. Woodbridge, Suffolk and Rochester, New York: The Boydell Press, 2005.

Kehew, Robert, ed. *Lark in the Morning: The Verses of the Troubadours*. Translated by Robert Kehew, Ezra Pound and W.D. Snodgrass. Chicago: The University of Chicago Press, 2005.

Martin, Sean. *The Cathars*. New York: Thunder's Mouth Press, 2004.

Nappholz, Carol Jane. *Unsung Women: The Anonymous Female Voice in Troubadour Poetry*. New York, Washington, D.C., Baltimore, San Francisco, Frankfurst am Main, Berlin, Vienna, Paris: Peter Lang, 1994.

Paden, William D. "The Troubadour's Lady: Her Marital Status and Social Rank." *Studies in Philology* 72 (1975): 28-50.
_____*The Voice of the Trobairitz : Perspectives On The Women Troubadours*. Philadelphia: University of Pennsylvania, 1989.

Poe, Elizabeth Wilson. "A Dispassionate Look at the Trobairitz." *Tenso*, Spring (1992): 142-164.

Pound, Ezra, *The Cantos*. New York: New Directions, 1923.

_____. *ABC of Reading*, New York: New Directions, 1934.

_____. *The Spirit of Romance*, New York: New Directions, and London: Faber and Faber, 1968.

Reiger, Angela. *Trobairitz: der Beitrag der Frau in der altokzitanischen höfischen Lyrik: Edition des Gesamtkorpus*. Tübingen: M. Niemeyer, 1991.

Rougement de, Denis. *Love in the Western World*. Princeton, New Jersey: Princeton University Press. 1983.

Robbins, Kittye Delle. "Woman/Poet: Problem and Promise in Studying the "Trobairitz" and their Friends." *Economia* 1.3 (1977).

Savall, Jordi. *Le Royaume Oublié: La Croisade Contre Les Albigeois*. Bellaterra España: Alia Vox, 2012.

Stoyanov, Yuri. *The Hidden Tradition in Europe*. London, New York, Victoria, Australia, Toronto, Canada, Auckland, New Zealand: Penguin Group, 1994.

Steiner, G. *After Babel: Aspects of Language and Translation*. 3rd edition. London, Oxford and New York: Oxford University Press, 1998.

Venutti, Lawrence. *Rethinking Translation: Discourse, Subjectivity, Ideology*. London and New York: Routledge, 1992.

_____. *The Translator's Invisibility: A History of Translation*. London and New York: Routledge, 1995.

_____. *The Scandals of Translation: Towards and Ethics of Difference*. London and New York: Routledge, 1998.

Weil, Simone. *Selected Essays: 1934-45*. Translated by Richard Rees. London, New York and Toronto: Oxford University Press, 1962.

Claudia Keelan is the author of six books of poetry, most recently the verse drama *O, Heart* (Barrow Street, 2014). Her honors include the Beatrice Hawley Award from Alice James Books (*Utopic* 2001) and the Jerome Shestack Prize from the *American Poetry Review* in 2007. *Truth of My Songs: The Poems of the Trobairitz* is her first book of translation. She is Professor of English and Director of Creative Writing at the University of Nevada, Las Vegas, where she edits the literary annual *Interim* (www.interimmag.org).

Truth of My Songs: Poems of the Trobairitz
by Claudia Keelan

Original cover art: *Allegro Moderato* © Aleksei Tivetsky and Elena Moross.
Courtesy of the artist.

Cover and interior text set in Warnock Pro.

Cover and interior design by Cassandra Smith

Each Omnidawn author participates fully in the design of his or her
book, choosing cover art and approving cover and interior design.
Omnidawn strives to create books that align with each author's vision.

Offset printed in the United States
by Edwards Brothers Malloy, Ann Arbor, Michigan
On 55# Enviro Natural 100% Recycled 100% PCW
Acid Free Archival Quality FSC Certified Paper
with Rainbow FSC Certified Colored End Papers

Publication of this book was made possible in part by gifts from:
Robin & Curt Caton
Deborah Klang Smith

Omnidawn Publishing
Richmond, California
2015
Rusty Morrison & Ken Keegan, Senior Editors & Publishers
Gillian Olivia Blythe Hamel, Managing Editor, Book Designer,
& OmniVerse Managing Editor
Sharon Zetter, Poetry Editor, Grant Writer & Book Designer
Cassandra Smith, Poetry Editor & Book Designer
Peter Burghardt, Poetry Editor & Book Designer
Melissa Burke, Marketing Manager & Poetry Editor
Liza Flum, Poetry Editor & Social Media
Juliana Paslay, Fiction Editor & Bookstore Outreach Manager
Gail Aronson, Fiction Editor
RJ Ingram, Poetry Editor & Social Media
Josie Gallup, Feature Writer
Sheila Sumner, Feature Writer
Kevin Peters, Warehouse Manager